GENERATIVE DEEP LEARNING
WITH PYTHON

UNLEASHING THE CREATIVE POWER OF AI

CUANTUM

THREE BOOK PROJECTS

1. FACE GENERATION WITH GANS
2. HANDWRITTEN DIGIT GENERATION WITH VAES
3. TEXT GENERATION WITH AUTOREGRESSIVE MODELS

First edition: May 2023

Published by Cuantum Technologies LLC.

Dallas, TX.

ISBN 9798395510143

"Artificial intelligence is the new electricity."

- Andrew Ng, Co-founder of Coursera and Adjunct Professor at Stanford University

CUANTUM
TECHNOLOGIES

Who we are

Welcome to this book created by Cuantum Technologies. We are a team of passionate developers who are committed to creating software that delivers creative experiences and solves real-world problems. Our focus is on building high-quality web applications that provide a seamless user experience and meet the needs of our clients.

At our company, we believe that programming is not just about writing code. It's about solving problems and creating solutions that make a difference in people's lives. We are constantly exploring new technologies and techniques to stay at the forefront of the industry, and we are excited to share our knowledge and experience with you through this book.

Our approach to software development is centered around collaboration and creativity. We work closely with our clients to understand their needs and create solutions that are tailored to their specific requirements. We believe that software should be intuitive, easy to use, and visually appealing, and we strive to create applications that meet these criteria.

This book aims to provide a practical and hands-on approach to starting with **Mastering the Creative Power of AI**. Whether you are a beginner without programming experience or an experienced programmer looking to expand your skills, this book is designed to help you develop your skills and build a **solid foundation in Generative Deep Learning with Python**.

Our Philosophy:

At the heart of Cuantum, we believe that the best way to create software is through collaboration and creativity. We value the input of our clients, and we work closely with them to create solutions that meet their needs. We also believe that software should be intuitive, easy to use, and visually appealing, and we strive to create applications that meet these criteria.

We also believe that programming is a skill that can be learned and developed over time. We encourage our developers to explore new technologies and techniques, and we provide them with the tools and resources they need to stay at the forefront of the industry. We also believe that programming should be fun and rewarding, and we strive to create a work environment that fosters creativity and innovation.

Our Expertise:

At our software company, we specialize in building web applications that deliver creative experiences and solve real-world problems. Our developers have expertise in a wide range of programming languages and frameworks, including Python, AI, ChatGPT, Django, React, Three.js, and Vue.js, among others. We are constantly exploring new technologies and techniques to stay at the forefront of the industry, and we pride ourselves on our ability to create solutions that meet our clients' needs.

We also have extensive experience in data analysis and visualization, machine learning, and artificial intelligence. We believe that these technologies have the potential to transform the way we live and work, and we are excited to be at the forefront of this revolution.

In conclusion, our company is dedicated to creating web software that fosters creative experiences and solves real-world problems. We prioritize collaboration and creativity, and we strive to develop solutions that are intuitive, user-friendly, and visually appealing. We are passionate about programming and eager to share our knowledge and experience with you through this book. Whether you are a novice or an experienced programmer, we hope that you find this book to be a valuable resource in your journey towards becoming proficient in **Generative Deep Learning with Python**.

Code Blocks Resource

To further facilitate your learning experience, we have made all the code blocks used in this book easily accessible online. By following the link provided below, you will be able to access a comprehensive database of all the code snippets used in this book. This will allow you to not only copy and paste the code, but also review and analyze it at your leisure. We hope that this additional resource will enhance your understanding of the book's concepts and provide you with a seamless learning experience.

https://books.cuantum.tech/gdl-python/code/

Premium Customer Support

At Cuantum Technologies, we are committed to providing the best quality service to our customers and readers. If you need to send us a message or require support related to this book, please send an email to **books@cuantum.tech**. One of our customer success team members will respond to you within one business day.

CLAIM YOUR
FREE MONTH

As part of our reward program for our readers, we want to give you a **full free month** of...

www.cuantum.ai

THE PROCESS IS SIMPLE

1 Go to Amazon and leave us your amazing book review

2 Send us your name and date of review to books@cuantum.tech

3 Join **cuantum.ai** and we will activate the Creator Plan for you, free of charge.

What is CuantumAI?

All-in-one AI powered content generator and money factory

A complete Eco-system

AI Powerded Chatbot Mentors - Templates - Documents - Images - Audio/Text Transcriptions - And more...

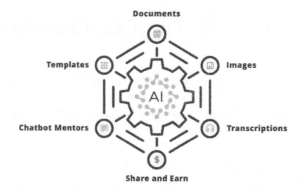

Get all your AI needs in one place to boost productivity, advance your career, or start an AI-powered business.

Do the research - Write the content - Generate the Image - Publish - Earn Money

CLAIM IT TODAY! LIMITED AVAILABILITY

TABLE OF CONTENTS

Introduction

Welcome, dear reader, to a journey through the exhilarating world of generative deep learning. This book is your passport to an adventure into one of the most transformative technologies shaping our world. As artificial intelligence (AI) continues to redefine the boundaries of what's possible, generative deep learning stands out as a profoundly powerful and exciting area of this evolving domain. It has the potential to shape and influence numerous facets of our lives and society, and this book is your guide to understanding and navigating this complex yet rewarding landscape.

Generative deep learning is a subfield of AI that focuses on models that can generate new, previously unseen data. It's an area where art and science intersect, where creativity meets technology. With applications ranging from creating realistic images, music, and text to generating novel chemical compounds for drug discovery, the possibilities are truly endless. By the time you reach the end of this book, you'll have a comprehensive understanding of generative deep learning and its vast potential.

In the chapters that follow, we start by laying a solid foundation. We will begin with the fundamental concepts and principles that underpin generative deep learning. This foundation is vital in ensuring a robust understanding of the field. Even if you are already familiar with some of these principles, this section will serve as a valuable refresher and provide a unified framework for the concepts that will follow.

As we delve deeper into the subject, we will explore a range of generative models, including Generative Adversarial Networks (GANs), Variational Autoencoders (VAEs), and Autoregressive models. Each of these models brings unique strengths and approaches to the task of data generation, and understanding their workings, strengths, and limitations is key to being able to apply them effectively.

The beauty of this book lies not just in the theoretical understanding it provides, but also in its practical, hands-on approach. Each chapter is supplemented with code examples, providing a practical understanding of the concepts discussed. These examples serve as a roadmap, guiding you in implementing and experimenting with these models yourself. The marriage of theory and practice is a defining feature of this book, and we believe it will greatly enhance your learning experience.

Beyond the fundamentals and the specific models, this book also ventures into the broader implications and applications of generative deep learning. We discuss how these models are used in various industries, the impact they're having, and the potential they hold for the future. This exploration is crucial in painting a comprehensive picture of the field and its significance beyond the technical domain.

As we near the end of our journey, we delve into the future landscape of generative deep learning. We discuss emerging trends, the potential impacts on various industries, ethical considerations, societal implications, policy, and regulatory outlooks. These discussions are crucial in understanding not just where the field is today, but where it's headed and the challenges and opportunities that lie ahead.

Learning, like any journey, is a process. There may be parts of this book that seem challenging, sections where you may need to pause and reflect, or even revisit. This is a natural part of the learning process, so we encourage you to take your time, ask questions, and be patient with yourself. Deep learning is a complex field, and mastery takes time and practice.

As we embark on this journey together, our hope is that this book will serve not just as a source of knowledge, but also as a source of inspiration. Generative deep learning is a field that thrives on creativity and innovation. As you delve into its depths, we hope you'll be inspired to think creatively, innovate, and contribute to this exciting field.

In conclusion, this book is more than just a guide; it's an invitation. An invitation to explore, to learn, and to create. It's an invitation to join the community of researchers, practitioners, and enthusiasts who are pushing the boundaries of what's possible with generative deep learning. So, buckle up, and let's embark on this exciting journey together. Welcome to the world of generative deep learning!

Chapter 1: Introduction to Deep Learning

Welcome to the exciting world of deep learning. In this chapter, we will introduce the basic concepts and principles that underlie deep learning. Whether you are a beginner in the field of artificial intelligence, or you have some experience and wish to deepen your understanding, this chapter will serve as a useful guide.

Deep learning is a subset of machine learning that's based on artificial neural networks with representation learning. It has revolutionized many industries by delivering superhuman accuracy with important applications like image recognition, voice recognition, recommendation systems, and more. Deep learning techniques can learn to perform tasks directly from images, text, and sound.

We will begin this journey with the basics of neural networks, which form the foundation of deep learning models.

1.1 Basics of Neural Networks

1.1.1 What is a Neural Network?

Artificial Neural Networks (ANNs) are a fascinating class of machine learning models inspired by the intricate workings of the human brain. ANNs are designed to process large amounts of data, identify patterns, and make predictions. They consist of a collection of connected nodes or 'neurons', each of which is capable of processing and transmitting information. The neurons are arranged in layers, hence the term 'neural networks'. ANNs have a wide range of applications, from image recognition to natural language processing. Whether you're working on a cutting-edge research project or developing a new product, ANNs are a powerful tool that can help you achieve your goals. In fact, as the field of artificial intelligence continues to grow and evolve, we can expect ANNs to become even more important in the years ahead.

In the world of machine learning, ANNs play a critical role in the development of deep learning models. Deep learning is a subset of machine learning that's based on artificial neural networks with representation learning. It has revolutionized many industries by delivering superhuman accuracy with important applications like image recognition, voice recognition, recommendation systems, and more. Deep learning techniques can learn to perform tasks directly from images, text, and sound.

As we dive deeper into the world of deep learning, it's important to understand the basics of neural networks, which form the foundation of deep learning models. ANNs are composed of layers of neurons that receive input signals and perform computations to produce output signals. Each neuron takes in multiple inputs, performs some computation, and gives an output. The connections between neurons carry weights, which are adjusted during the learning process. The goal of the learning process is to create a model that correctly maps the input data to the appropriate output.

In a neural network, the basic unit of computation is the neuron or node. Layers are composed of neurons, with an input layer that receives input features and an output layer that produces the final output. Between them, there can be one or more hidden layers. Each input into a neuron has an associated weight, which is assigned based on its relative importance. A bias is added to change the range of the neuron's output. The activation function decides whether a neuron should be activated or not. Common activation functions include the sigmoid, tanh, ReLU, and softmax.

As we continue our journey into deep learning, we'll explore more complex models and architectures that build upon these foundational concepts. We'll learn about the training process, understand how to tweak the model's parameters, and how to handle common challenges in building neural networks. This knowledge will serve as a solid base for your journey into generative deep learning.

Here is a simplified representation of a neural network:

```
Input Layer ----- Hidden Layer(s) ----- Output Layer
```

Code block 1

Each layer consists of multiple nodes or neurons, and each connection between nodes carries a weight, which is adjusted during the learning process. The goal of the learning process is to create a model that correctly maps the input data to the appropriate output.

1.1.2 Components of a Neural Network

1. Neurons

The basic unit of computation in a neural network is the neuron or node. It takes in multiple inputs, which can come from a multitude of sources such as sensors, other neurons, or external data. Each input is weighted according to its importance and then processed through an activation function, which determines the strength of the neuron's output. The output itself can be sent to other neurons in the network, where it will be further processed and used to make decisions. This complex web of interconnected neurons allows neural networks to perform highly sophisticated computations, from identifying images to translating languages.

2.Layers

A neural network is made up of layers that are interconnected to each other. These layers work together to produce accurate results. The input layer receives input features, which are then passed to the hidden layers. The hidden layers process the input and perform mathematical calculations to extract features that are then passed to the output layer. The output layer produces the final output of the neural network.

The number of hidden layers in a neural network depends on the complexity of the problem that it is trying to solve. In general, the more complex the problem, the more hidden layers will be required. However, adding too many hidden layers can cause overfitting, which can result in poor performance. Therefore, finding the right balance between the number of hidden layers and their complexity is an important part of designing an effective neural network.

In addition to the layers, neural networks also have weights and biases that are used to adjust the output of each layer. These weights and biases are initially set randomly, but are then adjusted through a process called backpropagation. Backpropagation is a method used to update the weights and biases of a neural network based on the error between the predicted output and the actual output.

The layers, weights, biases, and backpropagation are all important components of a neural network. By understanding how they work together, you can design and train neural networks that are effective at solving a variety of complex problems.

3. Weights and Bias

In neural networks, each input into a neuron has an associated weight, which is assigned based on its relative importance. The weights are adjusted during the training process in order to optimize the performance of the network. Additionally, a bias is added to change the range of the neuron's output.

This bias is also adjusted during training, along with the weights, in order to improve the accuracy of the network's predictions. By adjusting the weights and bias, neural networks are able to learn complex patterns and make accurate predictions on a wide range of tasks.

4. Activation Functions

The activation function is a crucial component in neural networks as it determines whether a neuron should be activated based on the input it receives. It serves as a non-linear transformer that allows for the neural network to learn complex patterns and relationships within data. There are various activation functions to choose from, each one with its own set of advantages and disadvantages.

For example, the sigmoid function is a common choice for binary classification tasks as it maps any input value to a probability between 0 and 1. The tanh function, on the other hand, is often used in image processing tasks as it maps input values to a range between -1 and 1, making it suitable for normalization. The ReLU function is a popular choice due to its simplicity and effectiveness in preventing the vanishing gradient problem. Lastly, the softmax function is often used in multiclass classification tasks as it produces a probability distribution over several output classes.

Overall, selecting an appropriate activation function is an important consideration when designing a neural network architecture as it can greatly impact the network's performance.

An Example of a Simple Neural Network

Here's a Python code snippet that uses TensorFlow and Keras to define a simple neural network with one hidden layer. We are using the **Sequential** API, which allows you to stack layers sequentially.

```python
from tensorflow.keras.models import Sequential
from tensorflow.keras.layers import Dense

# Initialize a sequential model
model = Sequential()

# Add an input layer with 8 neurons (features), and a hidden layer with 5 neuron
s
model.add(Dense(5, input_shape=(8,), activation='relu'))

# Add an output layer with 1 neuron
model.add(Dense(1, activation='sigmoid'))
```

Code block 2

In this example, we are using the rectified linear unit (ReLU) activation function in the hidden layer and the sigmoid function in the output layer.

It's important to remember that this is a basic introduction to neural networks. As we move further in this book, we'll explore more complex models and architectures that build upon these foundational concepts. We'll learn about the training process, understand how to tweak the model's parameters, and how to handle common challenges in building neural networks. This knowledge will serve as a solid base for your journey into generative deep learning.

1.1.3 The Perceptron: Building Block of Neural Networks

A neural network is made up of several neurons, which are also known as nodes or perceptrons. These neurons are the basic computational unit of the network and are designed to mimic the structure of neurons in the human brain. They are connected to one another and pass signals just like neurons in the human brain.

When designing a neural network, it is important to consider the structure of these neurons. The neurons receive inputs, which are then processed using a simple operation. The output of this operation is then passed to neurons in the next layer of the network. This process is repeated until the output layer of the network is reached.

While the structure of neurons in a neural network is based on the structure of neurons in the human brain, there are some key differences. For example, neurons in a neural network are not capable of thought or consciousness like human neurons are. However, they are still able to process information and make decisions based on that information.

The neuron is a key component of a neural network and understanding its structure and function is essential to designing an effective network.

Each input **x** to a neuron has a corresponding weight **w**, which is learned during the training process. The neuron calculates the weighted sum of its inputs, adds a bias **b** (also learned during training), and applies an activation function **f** to this sum to produce its output:

```
output = f(w1*x1 + w2*x2 + ... + wn*xn + b)
```

Code Block 3

Different types of activation functions can be used, depending on the problem at hand. Some of the most common ones include:

Sigmoid

The Sigmoid function is a mathematical function that is used to squashes values between 0 and 1. It is commonly used in binary classification problems, where the output of the model must be a probability value between 0 and 1. The sigmoid function is beneficial in such cases since it can map any input value to a probability value that lies between 0 and 1.

Furthermore, it is a smooth function, which means that it is differentiable, making it easy to use in gradient-based optimization techniques. Finally, the sigmoid function is also used in neural networks as an activation function, where it is used to introduce non-linearity into the model.

Tanh

Similar to sigmoid but squashes values between -1 and 1, thus centering the output around 0. The activation function is commonly used in neural networks due to its ability to prevent vanishing gradients. An issue with sigmoid is that it can cause the gradient to become very small, which can make learning difficult.

Tanh, on the other hand, has a steeper gradient and is able to learn faster. However, tanh also suffers from the same issue with vanishing gradients, especially when deeper neural networks are used. Despite this, it is still a popular choice for activation functions and is used in many state-of-the-art neural network architectures.

ReLU (Rectified Linear Unit): It keeps positive inputs as is and changes all negative inputs to zero. It is the most used activation function in CNNs.

Softmax

Softmax It is often used for multi-class classification problems as it gives a probability distribution over the classes. Softmax function is applied to a vector of real-valued numbers, and it maps the values to a probability distribution that sums up to 1. Its formula is $\exp(x[i])/\text{sum}(\exp(x[i]))$, where i is the index of the element in the vector, and x is the input vector. The resulting probability distribution can be used to predict the class of the input data point.

Multi-class classification problems

Multi-class classification problems are a type of supervised learning problems where the goal is to predict a target variable with more than two possible values. For example, predicting the species of a flower based on its characteristics is a multi-class classification problem. The Softmax function is a popular choice for solving multi-class classification problems because it can provide a probability estimate for each class.

Probability distribution

A probability distribution is a function that maps the values of a random variable to the probabilities of its possible outcomes. In the case of Softmax, the probability distribution is over the classes, and it assigns a probability to each one of them. The sum of all the probabilities of the classes is equal to 1, which means that the Softmax function outputs a valid probability distribution.

1.1.4 Backpropagation and Gradient Descent

One of the key algorithms used in training neural networks is backpropagation. Backpropagation is a gradient descent optimization algorithm that works by calculating the gradient of the loss function with respect to each weight in the network. This gradient is then used to update the weights in the opposite direction of the gradient, thereby minimizing the loss.

The learning rate is a hyperparameter that controls the amount by which the weights are adjusted during each iteration. A smaller learning rate results in more precise adjustments, but the training process may be slower. On the other hand, a larger learning rate speeds up the training process, but the adjustments may overshoot the optimal values, leading to less accurate results.

It is important to strike the right balance between the learning rate and the precision of the adjustments to achieve the best results. Additionally, there are various other techniques that can be used in conjunction with backpropagation, such as regularization and optimization methods, to further enhance the accuracy and performance of neural networks.

Here's a simplified description of the training process using backpropagation:

Forward Pass

The forward pass is the first step in the training of a neural network. During the forward pass, input data is fed into the network. Each layer computes an output based on its current weights and biases, and passes this output to the next layer. This process is repeated until the output layer produces the final output of the network.

The forward pass is an essential step in the training of a neural network, as it allows the network to make predictions based on the input data. By adjusting the weights and biases of the network during the training process, the accuracy of the network's predictions can be improved. In this way, the forward pass is a critical component of the machine learning process, enabling computers to learn from data and make predictions about the world around us.

Compute Loss

After the network's final output is produced, it is compared to the true output using a mathematical formula. The result is a loss value that serves as a measure of how far the network's predictions are from the actual truth. This process is essential for training the network to make more accurate predictions in the future.

The loss value is used to adjust the weights and biases in the network, which improves its accuracy over time. Deep learning models rely heavily on the ability to accurately compute loss, and it is a critical component of any successful machine learning project.

Backward Pass

During the backward pass, the network calculates the gradient of the loss with respect to each weight and bias by propagating the loss back through its layers. This step is crucial in updating the weights and biases of the network during the optimization process. The backward pass is a key component of the backpropagation algorithm, which is a widely used method for training neural networks.

By computing the gradients of the loss with respect to the weights and biases, the algorithm can adjust the network's parameters to minimize the loss function and improve the network's performance. Therefore, it is important to ensure that the backward pass is performed correctly and efficiently to achieve optimal results in training a neural network.

Update Weights

During the training process, the network learns to adjust each weight and bias to minimize the error between the predicted output and the actual output. This is done by computing the gradient of the loss function with respect to each weight and bias. The gradient tells us the direction in which we should adjust each weight and bias to decrease the loss.

We adjust each weight and bias in the opposite direction of its gradient using an optimization algorithm, most commonly gradient descent. By doing this repeatedly, the network gradually learns to make better predictions on new data.

This process is repeated for multiple iterations, or epochs, until the network's predictions are satisfactory.

Here's how to compile and train the previously defined model using the stochastic gradient descent (SGD) optimizer and binary cross-entropy as the loss function. We will use dummy data for the demonstration:

```python
from tensorflow.keras.optimizers import SGD

# Dummy input data
X_train = np.random.random((1000, 8))
y_train = np.random.randint(2, size=(1000, 1))

# Compile the model
model.compile(optimizer=SGD(), loss='binary_crossentropy')

# Train the model
model.fit(X_train, y_train, epochs=10)
```

Code block 4

In this simple code snippet, we first compile the model by specifying the optimizer and the loss function. The Stochastic Gradient Descent (SGD) optimizer is used to train the network, and the binary cross-entropy loss is appropriate as we're dealing with a binary classification problem in this example.

The **fit** function is then used to train the model for 10 epochs using our dummy input data (**X_train**) and the corresponding labels (**y_train**).

The number of epochs is a hyperparameter that determines how many times the learning algorithm will pass through the entire training dataset. One epoch means that each sample in the training dataset has had an opportunity to update the internal model parameters.

1.2 Overview of Deep Learning

1.2.1 What is Deep Learning?

Deep learning is a fascinating and rapidly expanding subfield of machine learning that focuses on developing and applying algorithms inspired by the structure and function of the brain. These algorithms, called artificial neural networks, are designed to be "deep" due to their complex network structure. The neural networks consist of multiple layers between the input and output layers, allowing for a more sophisticated analysis of the data.

Thanks to its foundation in neural networks, deep learning has been able to make significant strides in a wide range of fields. For example, deep learning has revolutionized computer vision, enabling computers to recognize and classify images with remarkable accuracy. Similarly, natural language processing has been transformed by deep learning, with cutting-edge algorithms able to understand

and generate human-like language. Deep learning is also making waves in audio processing, allowing computers to recognize and transcribe speech with greater accuracy than ever before. And in bioinformatics, deep learning is helping researchers to analyze complex biological data, leading to new insights and discoveries.

Deep learning is an exciting field with enormous potential. Its ability to learn from large amounts of data and make predictions based on that data is transforming the way we approach problems in many different domains. As researchers continue to refine and develop deep learning algorithms, we can expect to see even more impressive results in the years to come.

1.2.2 Why Deep Learning?

The rise and success of deep learning can be attributed to several factors. One of the main reasons is the significant advancement in computational hardware. Thanks to the advent of Graphical Processing Units (GPUs), deep learning models can now be trained much faster than before. Additionally, with the evolution of cloud computing, it's become more feasible to train large neural networks in a reasonable amount of time.

Another crucial factor is the availability of vast datasets. Deep learning models require massive amounts of data to be trained effectively, and with the explosion of the internet and the rise of connected devices, we now have access to more data than ever before. This abundance of data has enabled us to train deep learning models more accurately and effectively.

Furthermore, the development of new and improved training techniques has contributed to the success of deep learning. While neural networks have been around since the 1960s, it wasn't until the late 2000s that they became more popular due to better training algorithms and techniques. These new techniques include regularization, dropout, and batch normalization, to name a few.

In conclusion, the progress and development of deep learning are due to a combination of factors, including advancements in computational hardware, the availability of large datasets, and the development of new and improved training techniques.

1.2.3 Deep Learning vs Machine Learning

In machine learning, algorithms are designed to make predictions by learning from data. They do this by constructing a model of the data that captures relationships between the input and output variables. These models can be quite complex, with many layers of computations and parameters.

Deep learning, on the other hand, is a specific type of machine learning that trains a model to make classifications tasks directly from images, text, or sound. This capability is achieved through the use of deep neural networks, which are composed of many interconnected layers of nodes that allow for the extraction of high-level features from raw input data.

A significant advantage of deep learning models is that they often continue to improve as the size of your data increases. This is because deep learning models are capable of learning representations of the data that capture its underlying structure and dependencies. In contrast, traditional machine learning models might reach a plateau in performance, as they are limited by the capacity of their pre-defined feature representations.

In addition, deep learning models can be used for a wide range of tasks beyond classification, such as generation, translation, and reinforcement learning. These models have been applied successfully in fields such as computer vision, natural language processing, and game playing, among others. As such, deep learning represents a powerful and versatile tool for machine learning practitioners to tackle a variety of real-world problems.

1.2.4 Types of Deep Learning Models

There are various types of deep learning models, each with its specialty and type of data it's good at handling. Here are a few common types:

Feedforward Neural Networks (FNNs)

Feedforward Neural Networks (FNNs) are a type of artificial neural network in which information flows only in one direction, from the input layer, through the hidden layers, to the output layer. These networks are the simplest type of artificial neural network and are widely used in various applications, such as pattern recognition, image classification, and speech recognition. One of the advantages of feedforward networks is that they can be trained using supervised learning algorithms, such as backpropagation, which can help improve the accuracy of the network. Additionally, feedforward networks can be used in combination with other types of neural networks, such as recurrent neural networks, to create more complex models that can handle more complex tasks. While feedforward networks have certain limitations, such as the inability to handle temporal data, they remain an important area of research in the field of artificial intelligence.

Convolutional Neural Networks (CNNs)

CNNs are a specific type of neural network used for image processing tasks, such as image recognition. One of the key features of CNNs is their ability to automatically and adaptively learn spatial hierarchies of features. This means that they are able to identify patterns in an image and use that information to make more accurate predictions. CNNs are particularly useful when working with large amounts of data, as their ability to process information in parallel allows them to handle complex images quickly and efficiently.

CNNs consist of several layers, each with a specific function. The first layer is typically a convolutional layer, which applies a set of filters to the input image. This helps to identify key features in the image, such as edges or corners. The next layer is often a pooling layer, which reduces the dimensionality of the data by down-sampling the output from the previous layer. This makes the data easier to process and reduces the risk of overfitting.

Another important feature of CNNs is their ability to use transfer learning. This means that they can be trained on a large dataset and then adapted to a new task with minimal changes. This can save a significant amount of time and resources when working on a new project.

Overall, CNNs are a powerful tool for image processing tasks and have a wide range of applications in fields such as computer vision, medical imaging, and autonomous vehicles.

Recurrent Neural Networks (RNNs)

These are a type of neural network that is designed for sequential data, where the order and context of the data play a crucial role, such as in text processing and speech recognition. When compared to other types of neural networks, RNNs can work with input data of variable length, which makes them a good choice for tasks such as speech recognition, natural language processing, and time series analysis.

One of the key features of RNNs is their ability to maintain a memory of previous inputs, which allows them to take into account the context of the data when making predictions. This is achieved through the use of recurrent connections that allow information to be passed from one step of the sequence to the next.

RNNs are a powerful tool for sequential data analysis, and their applications are wide-ranging, from predicting the next word in a sentence to predicting stock prices over time.

Autoencoders (AEs)

AEs are a type of neural network that can be used for unsupervised learning of efficient codings. They are particularly useful for data compression, and can be used in a variety of applications, including image recognition and natural language processing.

Autoencoders work by learning an approximation to the identity function, so that the output is very close to the input. This is achieved by training the network on a set of input-output pairs, where the input is fed through the network and the output is compared to the input. The network is then adjusted to minimize the difference between the input and output.

One of the advantages of autoencoders is that they can be used for feature extraction. By training the network on a set of images, for example, the network can learn to extract relevant features from the images, such as edges and textures. These features can then be used for tasks such as image classification.

In addition to their use in data compression and feature extraction, autoencoders have also been used for anomaly detection. By training the network on a set of normal data, the network can learn to recognize when new data does not fit the normal pattern, indicating the presence of an anomaly.

Autoencoders are a versatile and powerful tool for unsupervised learning, with a wide range of applications in various fields.

Generative Adversarial Networks (GANs)

GANs are a class of deep learning models that are used to generate new, synthetic instances of data that are intended to be similar to real, existing instances. Unlike other traditional generative models, GANs generate new data by learning the underlying distribution of the real data.

This is achieved by training two neural networks: a generator network and a discriminator network. The generator network creates new data instances, while the discriminator network evaluates whether a given example is real or fake. The generator network's goal is to produce synthetic data that is indistinguishable from real data, and the discriminator network's goal is to correctly classify real and synthetic data.

Because of their ability to generate realistic images, GANs have become extremely popular in the field of image synthesis tasks, including the creation of photorealistic images, image-to-image translation, and even video synthesis.

Here is a simple example of creating a CNN model using TensorFlow and Keras:

```python
from tensorflow.keras.models import Sequential
from tensorflow.keras.layers import Conv2D, MaxPooling2D, Flatten, Dense

model = Sequential()

# Add the convolutional layer
# filters, kernel_size, activation_function, input_shape
model.add(Conv2D(32, (3, 3), activation='relu', input_shape=(64, 64, 3)))

# Pooling layer
model.add(MaxPooling2D(pool_size = (2, 2)))

# Second convolutional layer
model.add(Conv2D(32, (3, 3), activation='relu'))
model.add(MaxPooling2D(pool_size = (2, 2)))

# Flattening layer
model.add(Flatten())

# Full connection layer
model.add(Dense(units = 128, activation = 'relu'))

# Output layer
model.add(Dense(units = 1, activation = 'sigmoid'))
```

Code block 5

In the code above, we are constructing a Convolutional Neural Network (CNN) with two convolutional layers. Each convolutional layer is followed by a max-pooling layer, which reduces the spatial size of the representation, reducing the amount of parameters and computation in the network, and hence controlling overfitting. The flatten layer then transforms the 2D matrix data into a column vector which is fed to the fully connected layer (Dense layer). The output layer uses a sigmoid activation function to output a probability value for the binary classification task.

This was just a basic example of a deep learning model. Other architectures may include more layers, different types of layers, or even multiple interconnected networks. The choice of architecture will largely depend on the problem at hand.

Deep learning is a vast and exciting field, with new architectures and applications being published constantly. This is just the beginning of our exploration into the world of deep learning.

1.2.5 Challenges and Limitations of Deep Learning

While Deep Learning has proven to be an extremely powerful tool in many applications, it's important to note that it has several challenges and limitations:

Need for Large Amounts of Data

A significant amount of data is often required to train deep learning models effectively. This can be a challenge in cases where only limited data is available. One approach to addressing this issue is to use data augmentation techniques, which can help create synthetic data to supplement the existing dataset.

Another option is to use transfer learning, which involves using a pre-trained model as a starting point and fine-tuning it for the specific task at hand. Additionally, it may be possible to leverage data from related domains or sources to help increase the size of the training dataset. However, it is important to be cautious when doing so, as the quality and relevance of the additional data can have a significant impact on the performance of the model.

While the need for large amounts of data can be a challenge in deep learning, there are a variety of strategies that can be employed to help address this issue and improve model performance.

Computationally Intensive

Training deep learning models is often computationally expensive and could take a long time, especially when dealing with large networks and datasets. This is often mitigated by using specialized hardware like GPUs.

One of the reasons why deep learning models require such intense computation is because they are typically composed of many layers. Each layer processes information and passes it on to the next layer, and this process is repeated for many layers. Additionally, deep learning models often require a large amount of data to be trained on, and this data must be processed many times to ensure that the model is accurate.

This can result in long training times, which can be a major bottleneck in the development of new deep learning models. To address this issue, researchers have developed a variety of techniques to speed up the training process, such as using smaller batch sizes or applying regularization techniques. However, even with these techniques, training deep learning models remains a challenging and time-consuming task.

Model Interpretability

One of the most significant challenges in deep learning models is their "black box" nature. These models can generate high-quality output or make accurate predictions, but the internal workings that lead to these conclusions are often difficult to interpret and understand.

This lack of transparency, which is a common occurrence in deep learning models, can be a serious issue, particularly in fields where interpretability is critical. For instance, in the medical field, it is essential to understand how a model arrived at a particular diagnosis or recommendation.

Similarly, in finance, it is necessary to comprehend the rationale behind a model's prediction. Therefore, researchers and practitioners are continually exploring new techniques and methods to improve the interpretability of deep learning models, such as visualization, sensitivity analysis, and feature importance analysis, to name a few.

Overfitting

Deep Learning models have a tendency to overfit, especially when dealing with small datasets. Overfitting is when a model learns the training data too well and performs poorly on unseen data because it has failed to generalize from the training data. There are several methods to combat overfitting, including regularization, early stopping, and using larger datasets.

Regularization is a technique that adds a penalty term to the loss function to discourage the model from overfitting. Early stopping is a technique that stops the training process when the model starts to overfit. Using larger datasets can also help reduce overfitting by providing more examples for the model to learn from. However, collecting and labeling large datasets can be time-consuming and expensive.

Bias and Fairness

If the data used to train a model contains biases, the model will likely reproduce or even amplify these biases, leading to unfair outcomes. It is crucial, therefore, to ensure that the data used to train a model is as diverse and representative as possible, so that the model can learn to recognize patterns and make predictions that are not influenced by any particular group or demographic.

This means that data collection and preprocessing must be done with great care, and that the model itself must be designed to account for potential biases and to correct for them as much as possible. In addition, it is important to involve a diverse group of people in the model development process, so that a wide range of perspectives and experiences can be taken into account.

By doing these things, we can help ensure that machine learning models are as fair and unbiased as possible, and that they do not perpetuate or exacerbate existing inequalities in our society.

In conclusion, while Deep Learning offers powerful tools for many applications, careful consideration must be taken when deciding whether it's the right tool for the problem at hand. Furthermore, much ongoing research in the field is addressing these limitations, pushing the boundaries of what's possible with Deep Learning.

1.3 Practical Exercises

1.3.1 Theoretical Questions

1. What is the fundamental idea behind artificial neural networks?
2. Explain the difference between a neuron and an activation function.
3. What are the main reasons for the recent success of Deep Learning?
4. How does Deep Learning differ from traditional Machine Learning?
5. What are some challenges and limitations of Deep Learning?

1.3.2 Coding Exercises

1. Implement a simple perceptron in Python. You can use libraries like numpy for this. The perceptron should take an input, apply weights, add bias, and then pass the result through an activation function.

Example:

```python
import numpy as np

class Perceptron(object):
    def __init__(self, num_inputs, epochs=100, learning_rate=0.01):
        self.epochs = epochs
        self.learning_rate = learning_rate
        self.weights = np.zeros(num_inputs + 1)  # +1 for bias

    def predict(self, inputs):
        summation = np.dot(inputs, self.weights[1:]) + self.weights[0]
        return 1 if summation > 0 else 0

    def train(self, training_inputs, labels):
        for _ in range(self.epochs):
            for inputs, label in zip(training_inputs, labels):
                prediction = self.predict(inputs)
                self.weights[1:] += self.learning_rate * (label - prediction) *
inputs
                self.weights[0] += self.learning_rate * (label - prediction)
```

Code block 6

2. Using TensorFlow and Keras, implement a simple Feedforward Neural Network for a binary classification task. Use the dataset of your choice or a synthetic dataset created using libraries like Scikit-learn.

Example:

```python
import tensorflow as tf
from tensorflow.keras.models import Sequential
from tensorflow.keras.layers import Dense

# Define the model
model = Sequential()
model.add(Dense(10, input_dim=8, activation='relu'))  # input_dim=8 as we assume
input features are 8
model.add(Dense(1, activation='sigmoid'))  # binary classification, so one outpu
t node with sigmoid activation function

# Compile the model
model.compile(loss='binary_crossentropy', optimizer='adam', metrics=['accurac
y'])
```

Code block 7

3. Train the neural network from the previous exercise. Experiment with different numbers of epochs and observe how the model's performance changes.

Example:

We'll use a dummy dataset for this example.

```python
import numpy as np

# Dummy dataset
X_train = np.random.random((1000, 8))
y_train = np.random.randint(2, size=(1000, 1))

# Train the model
model.fit(X_train, y_train, epochs=10)
```

Code block 8

Here, the model will learn from the dummy dataset for 10 epochs. In practice, you would use a real dataset and split it into training and test sets to validate the model's performance. The number of epochs and the characteristics of the model (like the number of layers and nodes in each layer) are all hyperparameters that you can experiment with to optimize your model's performance.

These are very simplified examples intended to demonstrate the basic concepts. More complex models can be developed by adding more layers, using different types of layers, and using different techniques to optimize the model and prevent overfitting.

Please remember that the best way to learn is by doing. Trying to solve these exercises will deepen your understanding and proficiency in Deep Learning.

Chapter 1 Conclusion

In this introductory chapter, we've taken our first steps into the vast and exciting world of Deep Learning. We started with the basics of artificial neural networks, understanding the building block of these networks—the artificial neuron—and how the activation functions play a significant role in these networks.

We then delved into an overview of Deep Learning, where we saw what makes it different from traditional Machine Learning and why it's gained such popularity in recent years. We also explored various types of Deep Learning models, such as Feedforward Neural Networks (FNNs), Convolutional Neural Networks (CNNs), Recurrent Neural Networks (RNNs), Autoencoders (AEs), and Generative Adversarial Networks (GANs).

However, understanding Deep Learning is not just about knowing its capabilities. We also touched on the challenges and limitations associated with Deep Learning, such as the need for large amounts of data, computational intensity, issues with model interpretability, risk of overfitting, and bias and fairness concerns.

To reinforce these concepts, we concluded the chapter with practical exercises that offer a mix of theoretical questions and coding exercises. These exercises are designed to help you apply the knowledge you've gained and will continue to gain throughout this book.

Deep Learning is a continuously evolving field, with researchers around the world finding new ways to enhance the capabilities of deep learning models and tackle the limitations. With the fundamentals now under your belt, the subsequent chapters will delve deeper into specific architectures and their applications.

As we transition into the next chapter, we'll be exploring in detail a fascinating realm within Deep Learning—Generative Deep Learning. We'll uncover how these models can learn to create new content, whether it's an image, a piece of music, or even a block of text. Stay curious and keep exploring!

Chapter 2: Understanding Generative Models

Welcome to the second chapter of our journey, where we take a deep dive into the world of Generative Models. These models constitute an exciting subfield of Deep Learning and have received considerable attention in the past few years, thanks to their ability to generate new, previously unseen data that resembles the training data.

In this chapter, we will introduce the concept of generative models, explain why they're important, and discuss the various types of generative models, including Variational Autoencoders (VAEs) and Generative Adversarial Networks (GANs). We will also explore some of their exciting applications and how you can create and train your own generative models.

This chapter will offer a blend of theory and practice, with detailed explanations complemented by illustrative coding examples and exercises.

Let's start our exploration!

2.1 Concept and Importance of Generative Models

Generative models are a class of statistical models used in unsupervised learning that aim to learn the true data distribution of the training set so as to generate new data points with some variations. These models have shown great promise in various fields, such as image generation, text generation, and more.

Generative models are particularly useful in situations where there is limited data available, as they can be used to create additional data points that can be used for training machine learning models. Additionally, generative models can be used to create realistic simulations of complex systems, such as weather patterns or the behavior of large crowds.

Recent advances in generative models have also shown their potential in the field of medicine. For example, generative models can be used to create synthetic medical images that can be used to train deep learning models for diagnosing diseases. This can be especially useful in cases where obtaining real medical images is difficult or expensive.

Generative models are a powerful tool in the field of machine learning and have shown great promise in various applications. With further research and development, it is likely that we will continue to see the impact of generative models in many other fields as well.

2.1.1 What are Generative Models?

At the core, generative models are all about understanding the underlying data distribution. They attempt to model how the data is produced, aiming to capture the inherent structure and patterns. This is crucial because it helps us understand the underlying data in a more comprehensive way. Once trained, generative models can generate new data that resembles the training data, but it is not an exact replica.

For example, imagine you have a dataset of images of cats. A generative model trained on this dataset will try to understand the "cat-ness" in the images by learning aspects such as shapes, colors, and textures that make a cat a cat. This means that the model will be able to generate new images of cats that may not have been in the original dataset, but still exhibit the same cat-like characteristics. This is incredibly useful because it allows us to generate new data that is similar to the original data but expands the scope of the dataset.

In fact, generative models can be used in a variety of fields, including music, art, and literature. For instance, a generative model trained on a dataset of Shakespeare's sonnets can generate new sonnets that resemble Shakespeare's style. Similarly, a generative model trained on a dataset of classical music can generate new compositions that sound like they were composed by Beethoven or Mozart.

Generative models are a powerful tool that can help us understand data in a more comprehensive way and generate new data that expands the scope of the original dataset.

Example:

Let's consider a simple example. Suppose you have a dataset with a Gaussian distribution. A basic generative process could involve creating new data points that follow the same Gaussian distribution. Here's how you can do it with Python:

```python
import numpy as np
import matplotlib.pyplot as plt

# Assume we have a dataset with a Gaussian distribution
mu, sigma = 0, 0.1  # mean and standard deviation
s = np.random.normal(mu, sigma, 1000)

# Create a histogram
count, bins, ignored = plt.hist(s, 30, density=True)
plt.plot(bins, 1/(sigma * np.sqrt(2 * np.pi)) *
         np.exp( - (bins - mu)**2 / (2 * sigma**2) ),
         linewidth=2, color='r')

plt.show()
```

Code block 9

In this example, we first create a dataset **s** with a normal (Gaussian) distribution using numpy's **random.normal** function. Then, we visualize this data distribution using a histogram.

This is a very simple example of a generative process—creating new data points following a certain distribution. Generative models in Deep Learning involve much more complexity, including high-dimensional data, nonlinearities, and a need to learn the distribution from the data itself. We'll see examples of that as we move further into this chapter.

We can continue discussing the importance of generative models under the next subtopic, "2.1.2 Importance of Generative Models".

2.1.2 Importance of Generative Models

Generative models are significant for several reasons:

Data Generation

Generative models are a type of machine learning model that can create new data that looks similar to the training data. This can be incredibly valuable in situations where it is difficult or expensive to collect new data. For example, creating a dataset of images can be a time-consuming and resource-intensive process. However, a generative model can be trained on an initial set of images and then used to produce new, similar images. This can save a lot of time and resources while still allowing for the creation of a large dataset.

In addition to creating new data, generative models can also be used for tasks such as data augmentation and anomaly detection. Data augmentation involves creating new variations of the existing data to increase the size of the dataset. For example, a generative model could be used to create variations of an image by changing the color, brightness, or orientation. Anomaly detection involves identifying data points that are significantly different from the rest of the dataset. A generative model can be trained on the normal data and then used to identify anomalies that do not fit the expected patterns.

Generative models are a powerful tool for data generation and related tasks. They can save time and resources while still allowing for the creation of large datasets, and can be used for a variety of applications beyond just data generation.

Understanding Data Distribution

Generative models aim to learn the true data distribution, which can be a challenging task. By doing so, we can generate new data points that are similar to the ones in the original dataset, which can be useful in various applications, such as data augmentation.

Moreover, this understanding can be crucial in various tasks, such as anomaly detection, where we need to understand what constitutes "normal" data to identify anomalies effectively. For example, in medical diagnosis, we need to detect abnormal patterns in physiological signals to diagnose diseases accurately. By understanding the data distribution, we can identify these anomalies and make accurate diagnoses.

Another application of understanding data distribution is in data visualization. By understanding the underlying distribution of the data, we can create more informative and visually appealing visualizations that can help us gain insights into the data. We can also use this knowledge to identify potential biases in the data and take corrective actions to mitigate them.

Semi-Supervised Learning

A powerful application of generative models is in semi-supervised learning, where we have a large amount of unlabeled data and only a small amount of labeled data. In such a scenario, the generative model can significantly help improve performance on the labeled data. The generative model can learn from the large, unlabeled dataset and use that knowledge to make better predictions on the labeled data.

This approach is particularly useful in cases where labeled data is limited or expensive to obtain. In this way, generative models can provide a more cost-effective solution for improving performance in machine learning tasks. Additionally, the use of generative models in semi-supervised learning can also help reduce the risk of overfitting, which can be a common problem in supervised learning tasks.

Overfitting occurs when a model is too complex and learns to fit the training data too closely, leading to poor performance on new, unseen data. By leveraging the unlabeled data to learn more about the underlying structure of the data, the generative model can help reduce the risk of overfitting and improve generalization performance.

Thus, semi-supervised learning with generative models is a promising area of research that has the potential to significantly advance the field of machine learning.

Multi-modal Outputs

Generative models have the power to create multi-modal outputs, which means they can produce multiple types of output. One example of this is when the model is trained on a dataset that includes images of different kinds of fruits. Instead of only generating images of one type of fruit, the model can learn to create images of many different fruits.

These fruits might have different shapes, sizes, and colors. Furthermore, the model can be trained to generate other types of multi-modal outputs.

For instance, it could be trained on a dataset of speech recordings in different languages and learn to generate speech in any of those languages. Generative models are a powerful tool for creating complex, multi-dimensional outputs that can be useful in a variety of applications.

2.1.3 Generative Models vs. Discriminative Models

Machine learning is a fascinating field that involves the use of algorithms and statistical models to enable the computer to learn from data without being explicitly programmed. In this field, there are typically two kinds of models: generative models and discriminative models. Generative models aim to learn the underlying distribution of the data, which can be used to generate new samples from the same distribution.

Discriminative models, on the other hand, aim to learn the decision boundary that separates different classes of data. These two types of models have different goals and approaches to learning from data, but both are essential in machine learning and can be used for a wide range of applications such as image recognition, natural language processing, and speech recognition.

Generative Models

As we discussed earlier, generative models aim to understand the underlying data distribution. They learn how the data is generated, capturing the inherent structure and patterns. They then use this understanding to create new data points that resemble the training data. This can be a useful technique for various applications, such as generating realistic images or creating new music.

However, generative models can be computationally expensive and require a large amount of training data to work effectively. Additionally, there are various types of generative models, such as autoencoders and variational autoencoders, each with their own strengths and weaknesses. Despite these challenges, generative models are an important area of research in machine learning, and advancements in this field have the potential to revolutionize many industries.

Discriminative Models

In machine learning, there are two main types of models: generative and discriminative. As previously explained, discriminative models focus on the differences between classes and predict the class or label of an input. However, there are many different types of discriminative models that can be used for various purposes.

For example, some discriminative models are used for classification tasks, such as the classic example of a classifier that predicts whether an image is a cat or a dog. Other types of discriminative models can be used for regression tasks, time series analysis, or natural language processing. Despite their differences, all discriminative models share the common goal of accurately predicting the class or label of an input based on its features.

The key difference lies in their approach to learning. Generative models learn the joint probability distribution $P(X, Y)$ and use that to estimate the conditional probability $P(Y|X)$ for prediction. Discriminative models directly learn the conditional probability $P(Y|X)$.

While both types of models have their uses and advantages, our focus in this book is on generative models due to their ability to create new data and understand the intricacies of data distribution. This unique capability makes them suited for a range of fascinating applications, some of which we'll explore in later sections of this chapter.

With this understanding of the concept and importance of generative models, we're now equipped to delve into specific types of generative models in the next sections.

2.2 Types of Generative Models

Generative models are a fascinating topic in machine learning, as they can create entirely new data that resembles the original dataset. There are several types of generative models, each with their unique methodologies and strengths. In this section, we will focus on the two most prominent types of generative models: Variational Autoencoders (VAEs) and Generative Adversarial Networks (GANs).

VAEs are a type of generative model that uses a latent variable space to generate data. The model learns to encode the input data into a lower-dimensional space, and then decodes it back to the original space to generate new data. VAEs have been successful in generating realistic images, and they can also be used for data compression.

GANs, on the other hand, use two neural networks, a generator, and a discriminator, to generate new data. The generator tries to create data that resembles the original dataset, while the discriminator tries to distinguish between the real and generated data. GANs have been successful in generating realistic images and videos, and they have also been used for data augmentation.

Other types of generative models include Boltzmann Machines, Restricted Boltzmann Machines, and Deep Belief Networks. While these models are not as prominent as VAEs and GANs, they are still used in various applications.

Generative models are a fascinating area of study in machine learning, and there is still much to learn and discover about them.

2.2.1 Variational Autoencoders (VAEs)

Variational Autoencoders, or VAEs, are a type of generative model that uses ideas from autoencoders and infuses them with a touch of probability. This means that instead of learning a single fixed encoding for each input, a VAE learns a distribution of possible encodings. By making the encoding a probabilistic process, VAEs introduce a level of randomness that allows for the generation of novel outputs.

To achieve this, VAEs use an encoder-decoder architecture, just like autoencoders. The encoder compresses the input data and the decoder reconstructs the original data from the compressed form. However, in VAEs, the encoder outputs not a single fixed encoding, but rather a mean and variance for a distribution of possible encodings. This distribution is typically a normal distribution, with the mean and variance learned during training.

During the generation process, the VAE samples from this learned distribution to select a specific encoding for each input. This introduces variation into the output, allowing the VAE to generate novel data that is similar to the training data but not exactly the same. By learning a distribution of possible encodings, VAEs are able to capture the underlying structure of the data in a more flexible and nuanced way than traditional autoencoders.

In summary, VAEs are a type of generative model that learn a distribution of possible encodings for each input. This probabilistic approach introduces variation into the output, allowing the VAE to generate novel data that is similar to the training data but not exactly the same. By using an encoder-decoder architecture and a normal distribution to model the encoding, VAEs are able to capture the underlying structure of the data in a flexible and nuanced way.

Example:

To illustrate this concept, let's consider a very simple example of a VAE implemented using the Keras library in Python.

```python
from tensorflow.keras import layers
from tensorflow.keras import Model

# Define the size of our encoding space
encoding_dim = 32

# Define the input shape
input_img = layers.Input(shape=(784,))

# Define the encoder layer
encoded = layers.Dense(encoding_dim, activation='relu')(input_img)

# Define the decoder layer
decoded = layers.Dense(784, activation='sigmoid')(encoded)

# Define the autoencoder model
autoencoder = Model(input_img, decoded)
```

Code block 10

In the above example, we first define the size of our encoding space. Then, we define the input and the encoder and decoder layers. Finally, we define the autoencoder model. Note that this is a very simplified version of a VAE. Actual VAE models introduce a probabilistic aspect to the encoder and include a component called the 'reparameterization trick' to enable the model to backpropagate through the random sampling process.

2.2.2 Generative Adversarial Networks (GANs)

Generative Adversarial Networks, or GANs, are another type of generative model that have gained significant attention in recent years. Introduced by Ian Goodfellow and his colleagues in 2014, GANs consist of two neural networks – a Generator and a Discriminator – that are trained simultaneously and compete against each other (hence the term 'adversarial').

The Generator network generates new data instances, while the Discriminator evaluates them for authenticity; i.e. it decides whether each instance of data it reviews belongs to the actual training dataset or not. The generator is trained to fool the discriminator, and it wants to output data that look as close as possible to real, training data. Meanwhile, the discriminator is trained to correctly classify the data it receives as either real or fake.

The interplay between these two networks results in the generator network learning to generate data that are almost indistinguishable from the real data.

Example:

Here's a simplified example of how you might define the generator and discriminator networks in a GAN using Keras:

```python
from tensorflow.keras import layers
from tensorflow.keras import Sequential

# Define the generator
generator = Sequential()
generator.add(layers.Dense(256, input_dim=100))
generator.add(layers.LeakyReLU(0.2))

generator.add(layers.Dense(512))
generator.add(layers.LeakyReLU(0.2))

generator.add(layers.Dense(1024))
generator.add(layers.LeakyReLU(0.2))

generator.add(layers.Dense(784, activation='tanh'))  # Assume we're working with
28x28 grayscale images

# Define the discriminator
discriminator = Sequential()
discriminator.add(layers.Dense(1024, input_dim=784))
discriminator.add(layers.LeakyReLU(0.2))

discriminator.add(layers.Dense(512))
discriminator.add(layers.LeakyReLU(0.2))

discriminator.add(layers.Dense(256))
discriminator.add(layers.LeakyReLU(0.2))

discriminator.add(layers.Dense(1, activation='sigmoid'))  # Output a single valu
e representing whether the image is real or fake
```

Code block 11

In this example, both the generator and the discriminator are defined as simple feed-forward networks using the Sequential API in Keras. The generator takes a random noise vector as input and produces an image, while the discriminator takes an image as input and outputs a single value indicating whether the image is real or fake.

Please note that this is a very simplified example. In practice, GANs often use more complex architectures and training methods, especially for working with image data.

2.2.3 Other Types of Generative Models

While VAEs and GANs are the most prominent types of generative models, there are several other types worth noting. Some of these include:

1. **Autoregressive models**, such as PixelRNN and PixelCNN, generate data by modeling the probability of each element in the output given the previous elements.
2. **Flow-based models**, such as Normalizing Flows, model the data distribution using a series of invertible transformations to map the data to a known distribution.
3. **Energy-based models**, such as Boltzmann Machines, model the data distribution using an energy function that assigns a low energy to more likely configurations of the variables.

Each of these types of generative models has its own strengths and weaknesses, and the choice of model often depends on the specific task at hand.

With this understanding of the different types of generative models, we can now delve deeper into the specifics of VAEs and GANs in the following sections.

2.3 Training Generative Models

When it comes to training generative models, the ultimate goal is to make the model learn the parameters that will best capture the underlying distribution of the data. One of the most common techniques used for this purpose is stochastic gradient descent, which is an iterative optimization algorithm that allows the model to learn from the data by minimizing the loss function.

Essentially, the loss function is a mathematical tool that enables the model to evaluate the difference between the predicted output and the actual output. By minimizing the loss function, the model is able to adjust its parameters in such a way that it becomes more accurate in its predictions.

This section can be divided into the following subtopics:

2.3.1 Loss Functions

Generative models are an exciting area of research in machine learning. These models are often designed with unique loss functions that are used during training. One example of such a model is the Variational Autoencoder, which utilizes a combination of two loss functions: a reconstruction loss and a KL divergence loss.

The reconstruction loss is used to ensure that the model generates data that are similar to the training data, while the KL divergence loss helps the model to learn encodings that follow a specified distribution. This approach helps the model to generate realistic data that is similar to the training data while also being able to generate novel data points that are not present in the training set.

The use of unique loss functions allows for the creation of more complex and nuanced generative models that can be used to generate a wide range of data types, from images and videos to audio and text.

Example:

For VAEs, the loss function could be implemented as:

```python
from tensorflow.keras import backend as K

def vae_loss(x, x_decoded_mean):
    xent_loss = K.binary_crossentropy(x, x_decoded_mean)
    kl_loss = - 0.5 * K.mean(1 + z_log_var - K.square(z_mean) - K.exp(z_log_va
r), axis=-1)
    return xent_loss + kl_loss
```

Code block 12

Generative Adversarial Networks use a min-max loss function derived from game theory, which pits the generator and discriminator against each other in a two-player game.

The loss functions for the generator and discriminator in a GAN could be implemented as follows:

```python
def generator_loss(fake_output):
    return cross_entropy(tf.ones_like(fake_output), fake_output)

def discriminator_loss(real_output, fake_output):
    real_loss = cross_entropy(tf.ones_like(real_output), real_output)
    fake_loss = cross_entropy(tf.zeros_like(fake_output), fake_output)
    total_loss = real_loss + fake_loss
    return total_loss
```

Code block 13

2.3.2 Training Procedure

The training procedure for generative models often involves alternating between training different parts of the model. In VAEs, we alternate between forward propagation to compute the loss and backward propagation to update the model's parameters.

In GANs, we alternate between training the generator and the discriminator. The generator is trained to produce outputs that the discriminator mistakes as real, while the discriminator is trained to correctly classify real and fake instances.

A simplified GAN training loop could look something like this:

```python
def train_gan(generator, discriminator, data, epochs):
    for epoch in range(epochs):
        for images in data:
            noise = tf.random.normal([BATCH_SIZE, NOISE_DIM])

            with tf.GradientTape() as gen_tape, tf.GradientTape() as disc_tape:
                generated_images = generator(noise, training=True)

                real_output = discriminator(images, training=True)
                fake_output = discriminator(generated_images, training=True)

                gen_loss = generator_loss(fake_output)
                disc_loss = discriminator_loss(real_output, fake_output)

            gradients_of_generator = gen_tape.gradient(gen_loss, generator.trainable_variables)
            gradients_of_discriminator = disc_tape.gradient(disc_loss, discriminator.trainable_variables)

            generator_optimizer.apply_gradients(zip(gradients_of_generator, generator.trainable_variables))
            discriminator_optimizer.apply_gradients(zip(gradients_of_discriminator, discriminator.trainable_variables))
```

Code block 14

2.3.3 Challenges in Training Generative Models

Training generative models, such as GANs, can prove to be quite challenging due to a number of reasons. In GANs, for instance, there is a risk of the generator collapsing to producing the same output (mode collapse) or the discriminator overpowering the generator, leading to the generator not learning effectively.

These challenges often require the use of techniques such as regularization or the implementation of new loss functions to prevent the generator from collapsing or to ensure that the generator is learning effectively.

There are other challenges such as the choice of hyperparameters, the amount of data available, and the computational resources required to train these models. Despite these challenges, generative models remain a promising area of research, with many exciting applications in fields such as image and language generation, data augmentation, and anomaly detection.

2.4 Challenges and Solutions in Training Generative Models

Training generative models can be a challenging task due to several issues. One of the most prevalent problems that researchers encounter is mode collapse, which is when the model generates repetitive and limited samples. In addition to mode collapse, vanishing gradients is another issue that can cause the model's training to become unstable.

This is due to the fact that the gradients - which are used to update the model's parameters - can become very small and prevent further learning. Lastly, evaluating generative models is also a challenge. This is because there is no objective metric that can be used to assess the quality of the generated samples. As a result, researchers must rely on human evaluation, which is often subjective and time-consuming.

This section could cover the following subtopics:

2.4.1 Mode Collapse

Mode collapse occurs when the generator starts producing the same output (or a small set of outputs) over and over again. This can be due to the generator finding a particular output that fools the discriminator very well, leading the generator to produce variations of that output exclusively. This results in a lack of diversity in the generated samples.

Solutions to Mode Collapse

A commonly used solution to mode collapse is to use different types of GANs that encourage diversity in the outputs. For instance, Wasserstein GANs (WGANs) and Unrolled GANs have been shown to mitigate mode collapse to some extent.

2.4.2 Vanishing Gradients

Vanishing gradients can occur in GANs when the discriminator becomes too good at distinguishing real data from generated data. This results in the gradients that are backpropagated to the generator during training becoming very small, leading to the generator learning very slowly or not at all.

Solutions to Vanishing Gradients

Several solutions have been proposed to deal with the issue of vanishing gradients in GANs. One popular solution is to use different types of loss functions that provide stronger gradients when the discriminator is confident, such as the hinge loss or the least squares loss. Other solutions involve modifying the architecture of the generator and discriminator to make them less prone to vanishing gradients, such as using deep residual networks or normalization layers.

2.4.3 Evaluating Generative Models

Evaluating generative models is difficult as there is no straightforward way to measure how good the generated samples are. Commonly used metrics like Inception Score or Frechet Inception Distance only provide a coarse estimate of the quality and diversity of the generated samples and can be misleading.

Solutions to Evaluating Generative Models

While there is no perfect solution to the problem of evaluating generative models, using multiple metrics and qualitative evaluation (e.g., visual inspection of generated samples) can provide a more comprehensive view of the model's performance. It is also beneficial to use application-specific metrics when applicable. For instance, if the model is used for generating music, metrics that measure the musicality of the generated samples could be used.

2.4.4 Code Example

For instance, we can show how to use a different loss function, like the least squares loss, in a GAN to mitigate the vanishing gradients issue:

```python
# Least squares GAN loss
def generator_loss_LSGAN(fake_output):
    return tf.reduce_mean((fake_output - 1) ** 2)

def discriminator_loss_LSGAN(real_output, fake_output):
    return 0.5 * (tf.reduce_mean((real_output - 1) ** 2) + tf.reduce_mean(fake_o
utput ** 2))
```

Code block 15

In terms of model evaluation, we could provide code for computing common metrics like the Inception Score or Frechet Inception Distance:

```python
# Code for computing Inception Score
from scipy.stats import entropy

def inception_score(p_yx, eps=1E-16):
    p_y = np.mean(p_yx, axis=0)
    entropy_conditional = - np.sum(p_yx * np.log(p_yx + eps), axis=1)
    entropy_marginal = - np.sum(p_y * np.log(p_y + eps))
    IS = np.mean(entropy_marginal - entropy_conditional)
    return IS
```

Code block 16

These code snippets can help you understand how to implement some of the discussed solutions, but it's worth noting that you might need additional context and explanations in order to be useful in a real-world setting. For instance, you might need to know how to use TensorFlow's gradient tape to apply these custom loss functions, or how to obtain **p_yx** (the class-conditional probabilities) to compute the Inception Score.

2.5 Practical Exercises

The exercises in this section will provide you with ample opportunity to apply the concepts that you've learned in this chapter. You will have the chance to delve more deeply into the various types of generative models that you've been introduced to, explore their loss functions in greater detail, and work through some of the challenges that arise when training these models.

Specifically, you will be able to experiment with different techniques for fine-tuning your models, explore the use of regularization to prevent overfitting, and consider the various trade-offs that arise when selecting different hyperparameters.

The exercises will help you to develop a deeper understanding of how to apply the techniques that you've learned in a practical setting, by providing you with hands-on experience in working with real-world data. The skills that you develop through this section will help you to become a more effective practitioner in the field of machine learning, and to take on more advanced challenges as you continue to progress in your studies.

Exercise 2.5.1: Implementing a Variational Autoencoder (VAE)

In this exercise, you will implement a basic VAE in TensorFlow. The aim is to create a VAE that can generate new samples from the MNIST dataset.

Example:

Here's an example of how to implement a simple VAE in TensorFlow:

```python
from tensorflow.keras import layers

class VAE(tf.keras.Model):
    def __init__(self, latent_dim):
        super(VAE, self).__init__()
        self.latent_dim = latent_dim
        self.encoder = tf.keras.Sequential([
            layers.InputLayer(input_shape=(28, 28, 1)),
            layers.Conv2D(filters=32, kernel_size=3, strides=(2, 2), activation='relu'),
            layers.Conv2D(filters=64, kernel_size=3, strides=(2, 2), activation='relu'),
            layers.Flatten(),
            layers.Dense(latent_dim + latent_dim),
        ])
        self.decoder = tf.keras.Sequential([
            layers.InputLayer(input_shape=(latent_dim,)),
            layers.Dense(units=7*7*32, activation=tf.nn.relu),
            layers.Reshape(target_shape=(7, 7, 32)),
            layers.Conv2DTranspose(filters=64, kernel_size=3, strides=2, padding='same', activation='relu'),
            layers.Conv2DTranspose(filters=32, kernel_size=3, strides=2, padding='same', activation='relu'),
            layers.Conv2DTranspose(filters=1, kernel_size=3, strides=1, padding='same'),
        ])

    def encode(self, x):
        mean, logvar = tf.split(self.encoder(x), num_or_size_splits=2, axis=1)
        return mean, logvar

    def decode(self, z, apply_sigmoid=False):
        logits = self.decoder(z)
        if apply_sigmoid:
            probs = tf.sigmoid(logits)
            return probs
        return logits
```

Code block 17

Exercise 2.5.2: Implementing a Generative Adversarial Network (GAN)

Implement a GAN to generate new samples from the MNIST dataset. Pay particular attention to the loss functions of the generator and discriminator.

Example:

Here's an example of how to implement a simple GAN in TensorFlow:

```python
def make_generator_model():
    model = tf.keras.Sequential()
    model.add(layers.Dense(7*7*256, use_bias=False, input_shape=(100,)))
    model.add(layers.BatchNormalization())
    model.add(layers.LeakyReLU())
    model.add(layers.Reshape((7, 7, 256)))
    assert model.output_shape == (None, 7, 7, 256)
    # Continue adding layers...
    return model

def make_discriminator_model():
    model = tf.keras.Sequential()
    model.add(layers.Conv2D(64, (5, 5), strides=(2, 2), padding='same', input_sh
ape=(28, 28, 1)))
    model.add(layers.LeakyReLU())
    model.add(layers.Dropout(0.3))
    # Continue adding layers...
    return model
```

Code block 18

Exercise 2.5.3: Experimenting with Loss Functions

In this exercise, you'll modify the GAN you implemented in Exercise 2.5.2 to use a different loss function. Specifically, implement the least squares GAN loss and observe any differences in training and output quality.

Example:

Here's an example of how to implement the least squares GAN loss:

```python
def generator_loss_LSGAN(fake_output):
    return tf.reduce_mean((fake_output - 1) ** 2)

def discriminator_loss_LSGAN(real_output, fake_output):
    return 0.5 * (tf.reduce_mean((real_output - 1) ** 2) + tf.reduce_mean(fake_o
utput ** 2)
```

Code block 19

Exercise 2.5.4: Mode Collapse and Potential Solutions

In this exercise, we'll intentionally cause mode collapse in a GAN and then attempt to mitigate it. First, train a GAN on a diverse dataset but restrict the output size so that the GAN cannot reproduce the diversity of the input data. Observe the mode collapse. Then, implement one of the potential solutions to mode collapse discussed in this chapter, such as modifying the loss function or changing the model architecture.

Remember to experiment and explore different parameters, architectures, and techniques. The more you experiment, the better you'll understand the nuances of training generative models.

In the next chapter, we will go deeper into specific types of generative models and their applications. Stay tuned!

Chapter 2 Conclusion

In this chapter, we delved into the fascinating world of generative models. We started by understanding the concept of generative models and their importance in the world of deep learning. These models, as we learned, are capable of generating new, unseen data that share the same underlying patterns as the training data. This has far-reaching implications for a variety of fields, including art, entertainment, healthcare, and more.

We then looked at different types of generative models, including Variational Autoencoders (VAEs), Generative Adversarial Networks (GANs), and Autoregressive models. Each type has its unique strengths and characteristics that make them suitable for different types of problems.

Next, we dug into the nuances of training generative models, exploring concepts such as the likelihood, maximum likelihood estimation, and the evidence lower bound (ELBO). We learned how these concepts play a role in training our models and ensuring that they learn a robust representation of the data distribution.

Finally, we addressed some of the challenges that come with training generative models. Issues such as mode collapse and vanishing gradients can hamper the performance of our models, but we also discussed potential solutions to these problems.

The practical exercises at the end of this chapter were designed to help you apply these theoretical concepts. By implementing and experimenting with different types of generative models, you gain hands-on experience and a deeper understanding of the material.

In the next chapter, we'll dive into more details about Generative Adversarial Networks (GANs). We will explore their architecture, how they work, and how to implement them in TensorFlow. Stay tuned for more exciting insights into the world of generative models!

Chapter 3: Deep Dive into Generative Adversarial Networks (GANs)

In the previous chapter, we introduced generative models and briefly discussed various types of these models, including Generative Adversarial Networks (GANs). In this chapter, we will delve deeper into GANs and explore their architecture and training process in greater detail. We will also discuss the strengths and limitations of GANs and explore various applications that utilize these models, ranging from image synthesis to drug discovery.

To begin, GANs were introduced by Ian Goodfellow and his colleagues in 2014, and since then, they have had a significant impact on the field of deep learning. GANs are known for their ability to generate synthetic data that is incredibly realistic, making them useful in a variety of fields.

One of the key concepts we'll explore in this chapter is the architecture of GANs. GANs consist of two neural networks that work together: a generator network and a discriminator network. The generator network creates synthetic data, while the discriminator network evaluates how realistic that data is. Through an iterative training process, these networks work together to generate increasingly realistic synthetic data.

Another important topic we'll cover is the training process for GANs. GANs require a careful balance during training, as the generator and discriminator networks must be trained in tandem. We'll explore various techniques used in GAN training, such as adversarial loss and gradient descent.

In addition to discussing the architecture and training process of GANs, we'll also examine some of the challenges associated with using these models. GANs can be difficult to train and require a significant amount of computational resources. We'll also explore some of the variations of GANs, such as conditional GANs and Wasserstein GANs, and examine how they are used in real-world applications.

By the end of this chapter, you will have a comprehensive understanding of GANs and their workings, and be well-equipped to implement them using TensorFlow or other deep learning frameworks.

Let's start our exploration of GANs with an understanding of their foundation.

3.1 Understanding GANs

Generative Adversarial Networks (GANs) are an exciting development in the field of machine learning. They are composed of two main components: a Generator and a Discriminator. The Generator is responsible for creating synthetic data that is similar to the real data, while the Discriminator's job is to distinguish between the synthetic and real data. The two neural networks compete against each other in a zero-sum game framework, hence the term "adversarial."

GANs have many applications, from generating realistic images to creating new music and even developing video games. They have the potential to revolutionize many industries, including entertainment, healthcare, and finance. One of the key advantages of GANs is their ability to generate data that is similar to the real data, which is useful for training machine learning models. Another advantage is that they can generate data that is not limited by human imagination or creativity.

Despite their potential, GANs are not without their challenges. One of the main challenges is that they can be difficult to train, and it is not always clear what the best architecture or parameters are for a given application. GANs can suffer from mode collapse, where the Generator produces only a limited range of outputs, or from instability, where the Discriminator fails to distinguish between synthetic and real data.

GANs are an exciting area of research and development in the field of machine learning, with many potential applications and challenges to overcome.

3.1.1 The Generator

The Generator is a crucial component of the GAN (Generative Adversarial Network) architecture, which creates synthetic data that approximates the real data distribution. Its role is to take in a random noise vector as input and output data that can be used for training or testing machine learning models.

At the start of the training process, the Generator may create data that looks entirely different from the real data distribution, but as the network is trained, it gradually improves and begins to generate data that more closely resemble the real data. This process of generating synthetic data is important because it allows for the creation of larger datasets that can be used to improve the accuracy and robustness of machine learning models.

The Generator can be used to generate data that is similar to but not exactly the same as the real data, which can be useful in situations where privacy concerns prevent the use of actual data. Overall, the Generator is a powerful tool for data scientists and machine learning practitioners, enabling them to create more robust and accurate models that can be used in a wide range of applications.

Example:

Let's take a look at a simple implementation of a Generator in TensorFlow:

```python
def make_generator_model():
    model = tf.keras.Sequential()
    model.add(layers.Dense(7*7*256, use_bias=False, input_shape=(100,)))
    model.add(layers.BatchNormalization())
    model.add(layers.LeakyReLU())

    model.add(layers.Reshape((7, 7, 256)))
    assert model.output_shape == (None, 7, 7, 256)

    model.add(layers.Conv2DTranspose(128, (5, 5), strides=(1, 1), padding='sam
e', use_bias=False))
    assert model.output_shape == (None, 7, 7, 128)
    model.add(layers.BatchNormalization())
    model.add(layers.LeakyReLU())

    # Further layers are added here...

    return model
```

Code block 20

This is a simple generator model using TensorFlow's Keras API. The generator starts with a dense layer taking a random noise vector as input and then reshapes it to a 7x7x256 tensor. It then uses transpose convolutions (also known as deconvolutions) to upscale this tensor and generate an image.

3.1.2 The Discriminator

The Discriminator's role in the GAN framework is of utmost importance, as it serves as a binary classifier to distinguish between the "real" data from the actual dataset and "fake" data generated by the generator. In the initial stages of training, the discriminator is fed both real and fake data and tries to classify them correctly.

This process is repeated several times to help the discriminator gain a better understanding of what real data looks like and how to distinguish it from the artificial data generated by the generator. It is important to note that the discriminator's performance is crucial in determining the quality of the generator's output. Therefore, a well-trained discriminator is essential in producing high-quality synthetic data that closely resembles real-world data.

Example:

Here is a simple example of a Discriminator using TensorFlow:

```python
def make_discriminator_model():
    model = tf.keras.Sequential()
    model.add(layers.Conv2D(64, (5, 5), strides=(2, 2), padding='same', input_sh
ape=[28, 28, 1]))
    model.add(layers.LeakyReLU())
    model.add(layers.Dropout(0.3))

    model.add(layers.Conv2D(128, (5, 5), strides=(2, 2), padding='same'))
    model.add(layers.LeakyReLU())
    model.add(layers.Dropout(0.3))

    model.add(layers.Flatten())
    model.add(layers.Dense(1))

    return model
```

Code block 21

In this example, the Discriminator is a simple Convolutional Neural Network (CNN) model. It starts with a convolutional layer that reduces the spatial dimensions of the input, followed by a LeakyReLU activation and a Dropout layer for regularization. This process is repeated, and finally, a dense layer is used to output a single value that classifies the input as real or fake.

This is a high-level overview of how GANs work. In the next sections, we will delve deeper into the components of GANs, their training process, and how they manage to generate realistic data.

3.1.3 GAN Training and Objective Function

Generative Adversarial Networks (GANs) are a type of machine learning algorithm that consists of two neural networks: the generator and the discriminator. In GANs, the generator and the discriminator are trained in tandem in a sort of tug-of-war game. This adversarial process is what makes GANs so unique and effective.

The generator is trying to generate synthetic data that the discriminator can't distinguish from real data. Its goal is not only to maximize the chance that the discriminator makes a mistake in classification, but also to create variations of the original data that the discriminator has never seen before. In other words, the generator is trying to capture the underlying distribution of the real data and generate new samples that are consistent with that distribution.

On the other hand, the discriminator is trying to get better at distinguishing between real and fake data. It wants to minimize the chance that it classifies a sample incorrectly. To achieve this, the discriminator needs to learn the features that are most relevant for distinguishing between real and fake data. As the generator improves, the discriminator needs to become more discerning in order to maintain the same level of accuracy.

This dynamic interplay between the generator and discriminator is what drives the learning process in GANs. As they play this game of cat and mouse, the generator becomes better at generating realistic data, while the discriminator becomes more adept at identifying fake data. The end result is a generator that can produce high-quality synthetic data that is indistinguishable from real data, and a discriminator that can accurately detect fake data with a high degree of confidence.

This training process can be defined by the following value (or objective) function:

min_G max_D V(D, G) = E[log(D(x))] + E[log(1 - D(G(z)))]

In simpler terms, this value function says:

1. We want to maximize D's ability to correctly classify real and fake samples (**max_D**). This is done by increasing the value of **log(D(x))** (the log-probability that real data x is real) and **log(1 - D(G(z)))** (the log-probability that fake data is fake).
2. We want to minimize G's ability to fool D (**min_G**). This is done by trying to reduce the value of **log(1 - D(G(z)))** (the log-probability that fake data is fake).

In practice, this is done in alternating steps:

- In one step, the generator is frozen and the discriminator is trained on a batch of real and a batch of generated samples.
- In the next step, the discriminator is frozen and the generator is updated in a direction that makes the generated samples more likely to be classified as real by the discriminator.

This adversarial training process, albeit tricky to get right, results in a generator that can produce samples that closely mimic the distribution of the real data.

3.2 Architecture of GANs

GANs, or Generative Adversarial Networks, are a type of neural network composed of two interconnected sub-networks, the generator and discriminator. The generator produces synthetic data, while the discriminator evaluates the authenticity of the generated data. This unique architecture is what makes GANs so effective in image generation, video synthesis, and other creative tasks.

The generator network, as its name implies, generates synthetic data by learning from real data. It does this by mapping the input noise vector to a space where the data resides. The discriminator network, on the other hand, takes in both real and synthetic data and tries to distinguish between them. The goal of the generator is to produce synthetic data that is so similar to the real data that the discriminator cannot tell the difference.

As a result of this adversarial training, GANs have the ability to generate high-quality, realistic data that closely resembles the real data. This makes them useful in a variety of applications, such as image and video synthesis, data augmentation, and more. It is important to note that while GANs have shown great success in these areas, they can still suffer from issues such as mode collapse and instability. These issues are actively being researched and addressed by the machine learning community.

3.2.1 Generator

A key component of a Generative Adversarial Network (GAN) is its generator. The generator's primary task is to create new, synthetic data that emulates the distribution of the real data as closely as possible. To accomplish this, the generator takes a latent space vector as input and outputs data that should resemble the real data.

The architecture of the generator is critical in determining the quality and realism of the generated data. Depending on the type of data you are trying to generate, the architecture of the generator will vary. For example, if you're generating images, a popular approach is to use a deep convolutional neural network (CNN) with upsampling layers. In contrast, if you're generating music, you might use a recurrent neural network (RNN) with long short-term memory (LSTM) cells.

The generator plays a critical role in the success of a GAN, and its architecture must be carefully designed to ensure the synthetic data is of high quality and resembles the real data as closely as possible.

Code example: Image Generator

Let's take the example of generating images. The architecture of a generator for an image GAN (such as DCGAN) would typically be a series of transpose convolutional layers. Here's a simple generator model using TensorFlow's Keras API:

```python
def make_generator_model():
    model = tf.keras.Sequential()

    model.add(layers.Dense(7*7*256, use_bias=False, input_shape=(100,)))
    model.add(layers.BatchNormalization())
    model.add(layers.LeakyReLU())

    model.add(layers.Reshape((7, 7, 256)))

    model.add(layers.Conv2DTranspose(128, (5, 5), strides=(1, 1), padding='sam
e', use_bias=False))
    model.add(layers.BatchNormalization())
    model.add(layers.LeakyReLU())

    model.add(layers.Conv2DTranspose(64, (5, 5), strides=(2, 2), padding='same',
use_bias=False))
    model.add(layers.BatchNormalization())
    model.add(layers.LeakyReLU())

    model.add(layers.Conv2DTranspose(1, (5, 5), strides=(2, 2), padding='same',
use_bias=False, activation='tanh'))

    return model
```

Code block 22

This model takes a noise vector of size 100 as input and produces a 28x28 grayscale image. The LeakyReLU activations and batch normalization layers help stabilize the training process.

3.2.2 Discriminator

In a Generative Adversarial Network (GAN), the discriminator represents a binary classifier responsible for distinguishing between the real and fake data. The generator produces samples of data and the discriminator evaluates them based on their similarity to the real data. By doing so, the discriminator provides feedback to the generator to improve the realism of the generated data.

This process is repeated many times until the generator produces samples that are indistinguishable from the real data, creating a realistic simulation of the original data. In this way, the discriminator plays a critical role in the GAN by training the generator to produce high-quality data.

Code example: Image Discriminator

In an image GAN, the discriminator would typically be a standard convolutional neural network that ends with a dense layer outputting a single value. Here's an example of a discriminator model:

```python
def make_discriminator_model():
    model = tf.keras.Sequential()

    model.add(layers.Conv2D(64, (5, 5), strides=(2, 2), padding='same', input_sh
ape=[28, 28, 1]))
    model.add(layers.LeakyReLU())
    model.add(layers.Dropout(0.3))

    model.add(layers.Conv2D(128, (5, 5), strides=(2, 2), padding='same'))
    model.add(layers.LeakyReLU())
    model.add(layers.Dropout(0.3))

    model.add(layers.Flatten())
    model.add(layers.Dense(1))

    return model
```

Code block 23

This model takes a 28x28 grayscale image as input and outputs a single value that signifies whether the input image is real (from the dataset) or fake (generated).

These are the key components of a GAN. In the next section, we'll discuss the training process and how these components interact to produce a model that can generate realistic data.

3.2.3 Variations in GAN Architecture

GANs are incredibly flexible in terms of architecture. There are dozens of GAN variants that tweak the base architecture to improve performance or to generate different kinds of data.

Deep Convolutional GANs (DCGANs):

Deep Convolutional GANs (DCGANs) are considered one of the most popular GAN architectures used in machine learning. They are especially suited to image data analysis due to their use of convolutional layers in both the generator and the discriminator. This allows for a more accurate representation of the image data, resulting in higher quality output.

In addition to their use of convolutional layers, DCGANs introduced architectural guidelines to contribute to stable training. These guidelines include the use of strided convolutions instead of pooling layers, batch normalization, and ReLU activations in the generator and LeakyReLU activations in the discriminator. DCGANs are a significant advancement in the field of machine learning and have been used to generate realistic images of faces, animals, and even landscapes.

Conditional GANs (cGANs)

While the basic GAN model generates data from random noise, conditional GANs allow for the generation of data with specific characteristics. They work by conditioning the model on additional information, like a class label, which guides the data generation process.

This means that, unlike basic GANs which can only generate data from random noise, cGANs have the ability to generate data with specific attributes. For example, if a cGAN is trained on a dataset of images of animals and their respective classifications, it can generate images of animals with specific classifications. This makes cGANs a powerful tool in image generation for various applications such as in the field of computer vision.

Another use case for cGANs is in the generation of realistic images for data augmentation. By conditioning the model on the characteristics of the image dataset, the cGAN can generate new images that are similar to the original dataset, but with subtle differences. This can be helpful in creating larger datasets for training machine learning models, which can improve their accuracy and generalization ability.

Overall, conditional GANs are a valuable extension of the basic GAN model that enable data generation with specific attributes, making them a powerful tool in various fields such as computer vision and machine learning.

Wasserstein GANs (WGANs)

Wasserstein GANs (WGANs) is a type of generative adversarial network (GAN) that proposes a new objective function derived from the Wasserstein distance. This is different from the original GANs which use the JS divergence.

The Wasserstein distance is a mathematical concept that measures the distance between two probability distributions. It has the advantage of being able to handle distributions with disjoint supports. This is particularly useful in image generation tasks where the generator may generate images that are not in the same space as the real images.

Using the Wasserstein distance as the basis for the objective function leads to more stable training and helps mitigate issues like mode collapse. Mode collapse is a common problem in GANs where the generator produces a limited set of outputs, failing to capture the full diversity of the target distribution.

Wasserstein GANs are a promising advancement in the field of generative models, providing a more stable and effective training method for image generation tasks.

CycleGANs

CycleGANs are an impressive and innovative architecture that have been developed in recent years. They are an important breakthrough in the field of computer vision, and have the potential to revolutionize the way we think about image-to-image translation. With CycleGANs, it is now possible to translate images from one domain to another, without needing explicit pairings in the training data.

This means that we can now translate images of horses to zebras, or summer landscapes to winter, with ease and accuracy. Furthermore, CycleGANs have been shown to be highly effective at a range of other tasks, such as style transfer, image colorization, and more. Overall, CycleGANs represent a major step forward in the field of computer vision, and are sure to be the focus of much excitement and innovation in the years to come.

StackGANs

StackGANs are an innovative deep learning architecture that utilizes natural language processing to generate high-quality images from textual descriptions. This technology consists of a two-stage process: the first stage utilizes a text encoder to generate a low-resolution image from a given text description, and the second stage utilizes an image encoder to produce a high-resolution image that is both realistic and visually pleasing.

The primary advantage of StackGANs is their ability to learn from complex textual descriptions and generate images that accurately depict the described objects or scenes. This technology has numerous applications in industries such as fashion, entertainment, and advertising, where realistic high-quality images are essential. Furthermore, this technology has the potential to revolutionize the way we create and disseminate visual content, allowing us to generate high-quality images at scale and with minimal human intervention.

These are just a few examples. The field of GANs is actively researched and new architectures and training methods are constantly being proposed. Each variant has its own strengths and is suited to different tasks, but they all share the basic GAN architecture of a generator and a discriminator network playing a minimax game.

3.3 Training GANs

Training Generative Adversarial Networks (GANs) can be a complex and fascinating process. This is because it involves an iterative competition between two models: a generator and a discriminator. The generator attempts to create fake data that can pass as real data, while the discriminator tries to distinguish between the real and fake data produced by the generator. This iterative competition can result in the generator producing increasingly realistic fake data, while the discriminator becomes better at identifying fake data.

There are several methods that are commonly used to train GANs effectively. One such method is called the Wasserstein GAN (WGAN), which uses a different loss function than the traditional GAN. The WGAN loss function helps to address some of the issues that arise when training traditional GANs, such as mode collapse. Another method is the use of conditional GANs, which allow the generator to take in additional information, such as class labels, to create more specific fake data. These are just a few examples of the methods that are used to train GANs effectively.

In this section, we will explore the complexities of the GAN training process in more detail, and discuss these and other methods used to train GANs effectively. By the end of this section, you will have a better understanding of the challenges involved in training GANs, as well as the techniques used to overcome them.

3.3.1 The Basic Training Process

Generative Adversarial Networks (GANs) are a type of neural network that is trained using a two-player minimax game. This game involves a competition between two players, one of whom tries to maximize a certain quantity while the other tries to minimize it.

The goal of GANs is to generate realistic data that is similar to the training data, but not identical to it. To achieve this, GANs use a generator network that generates new data samples, and a discriminator network that tries to distinguish between the generated data and the real data. The two networks are trained together in a process called adversarial training, where the generator tries to fool the discriminator, and the discriminator tries to correctly identify the generated data.

This process continues until the generator produces data that is indistinguishable from the real data, at which point the training process is complete. GANs have been used for a variety of applications, including image and video generation, data augmentation, and data privacy.

Here's how the process works in broad strokes:

1. **Step 1:** The generator creates fake data by taking random noise as input and producing data in the desired domain (e.g., images).

2. **Step 2:** The discriminator takes in both real data (from the training set) and the fake data produced by the generator. It then makes predictions about whether each piece of data is real or fake.

3. **Step 3:** Both models are updated based on the discriminator's performance. The discriminator is trained to maximize the probability of correctly classifying real and fake data, while the generator is trained to maximize the probability that the discriminator makes mistakes.

Let's take a look at what this might look like in terms of code.

Code example: Training a GAN

Here is a simplified version of the training loop for a GAN, assuming you already have a generator and a discriminator (like the ones we created earlier):

```python
# This method returns a helper function to compute cross entropy loss
cross_entropy = tf.keras.losses.BinaryCrossentropy(from_logits=True)

def discriminator_loss(real_output, fake_output):
    real_loss = cross_entropy(tf.ones_like(real_output), real_output)
    fake_loss = cross_entropy(tf.zeros_like(fake_output), fake_output)
    total_loss = real_loss + fake_loss
    return total_loss

def generator_loss(fake_output):
    return cross_entropy(tf.ones_like(fake_output), fake_output)

generator_optimizer = tf.keras.optimizers.Adam(1e-4)
discriminator_optimizer = tf.keras.optimizers.Adam(1e-4)

@tf.function
def train_step(images):
    noise = tf.random.normal([BATCH_SIZE, 100])

    with tf.GradientTape() as gen_tape, tf.GradientTape() as disc_tape:
        generated_images = generator(noise, training=True)

        real_output = discriminator(images, training=True)
        fake_output = discriminator(generated_images, training=True)

        gen_loss = generator_loss(fake_output)
        disc_loss = discriminator_loss(real_output, fake_output)

    gradients_of_generator = gen_tape.gradient(gen_loss, generator.trainable_var
iables)
    gradients_of_discriminator = disc_tape.gradient(disc_loss, discriminator.tra
inable_variables)

    generator_optimizer.apply_gradients(zip(gradients_of_generator, generator.tr
ainable_variables))
    discriminator_optimizer.apply_gradients(zip(gradients_of_discriminator, disc
riminator.trainable_variables))
```

Code block 24

In this code, we use binary cross entropy as our loss function. The generator's loss quantifies how well it was able to trick the discriminator. Intuitively, if the generator is performing well, the discriminator will classify the fake images as real (or 1). Here, we compare the discriminator's decisions on the generated images to an array of 1s.

The discriminator's loss is calculated as the sum of the loss for the real and fake images. The real_loss is a sigmoid cross entropy loss of the real images and an array of ones (since these are the real images). The fake_loss is a sigmoid cross entropy loss of the fake images and an array of zeros (since these are the fake images). The discriminator's total loss is the sum of real_loss and the fake_loss. In other words, the discriminator's loss is low when it correctly classifies real images as real and fake images as fake.

In the training loop, we first generate images with our generator from random noise. Then we pass both real images from our training set and the generated images to the discriminator, obtaining the real_output and fake_output respectively. The losses for the generator and discriminator are calculated separately using the functions we defined above, and then we use gradient descent to update the weights of the generator and discriminator in the direction that minimizes their respective loss.

It's important to note that the generator and discriminator are trained simultaneously: we do one step of discriminator training for each step of generator training. This allows both the generator and the discriminator to gradually improve over time.

While this training process can work, it often runs into problems in practice. In the next sub-sections, we'll cover some of these common issues, as well as strategies to mitigate them.

3.3.2 Common Training Problems and Possible Solutions

Although GANs have the potential to generate impressive results, their training process is often challenging and prone to multiple issues. Specifically, the interplay between the generator and discriminator models can result in several problems, such as the mode collapse phenomenon, which happens when the generator produces the same output for multiple input values, or vanishing gradients, which can occur when the gradients of the discriminator become too small, hindering the generator's learning process.

The instability of GANs can lead to problems such as oscillations between the discriminator and generator, which can significantly affect the quality of the generated outputs. Therefore, while GANs have proven to be a powerful tool for generating realistic data, their training process requires careful consideration and management to ensure optimal results.

Let's discuss these problems in more detail, and explore some potential solutions.

Mode Collapse

Mode collapse happens when the generator produces a limited diversity of samples, or even the same sample, regardless of the input noise. This is often a result of the generator finding a loophole in the discriminator's strategy. Once the generator finds a type of sample that can fool the discriminator, it might stick to generating that type of sample, ignoring other possible outputs.

Solution: A common solution to mode collapse is introducing some randomness into the discriminator's feedback to the generator. This can be done by adding noise to the discriminator's output or the labels used for training. This makes it harder for the generator to exploit the discriminator's strategy, promoting a more diverse range of outputs.

Vanishing Gradients

Vanishing gradients can occur when the discriminator becomes too good. If the discriminator's performance is perfect or near-perfect, the generator's gradient can vanish, making it difficult for the generator to improve.

Solution: One solution is to modify the loss function used for training the generator. Instead of trying to maximize the probability that the generated samples are classified as real, the generator can be trained to minimize the probability that they are classified as fake. This change in perspective can help mitigate the problem of vanishing gradients.

Instability

The training of GANs can be unstable because the generator and discriminator are trained simultaneously and they can affect each other's learning process. For example, if the generator improves rapidly, the discriminator's performance can degrade, making its feedback less useful for the generator.

Solution: Several strategies have been proposed to deal with this problem. One approach is to use different learning rates for the generator and the discriminator. Another approach is to occasionally freeze the training of one model while the other one catches up. Techniques like gradient clipping or spectral normalization can also help stabilize the training.

Remember, these solutions are not silver bullets, and they may not completely eliminate the problems they are designed to address. However, they can make the training process more manageable and increase the likelihood of obtaining a well-performing GAN model.

3.3.3 Advanced Techniques

In addition to the standard GAN architecture and training approach, there have been numerous modifications and enhancements proposed to further improve the quality of the generated samples and stabilize the training process.

For instance, some researchers have introduced regularization terms to the loss function to encourage the generator to produce diverse samples. Others have proposed using different architectures for the generator and discriminator, such as Wasserstein GANs and CycleGANs.

Some have even explored using multiple discriminators to provide more detailed feedback to the generator. Despite these advancements, challenges still remain in training and optimizing GANs, such as mode collapse and vanishing gradients. Further research and experimentation are needed to overcome these obstacles and fully unleash the potential of GANs in various applications.

These include variations like:

Conditional GANs

These are GANs that can generate data according to specific conditions, such as class labels or other modalities of data. This allows for more targeted and specific generation of data that can be useful in a variety of applications.

For example, conditional GANs can be used in image generation to create images of a certain category, such as dogs or cars, based on the input of a specific label. They can also be used in text generation to generate text based on a specific prompt or topic.

The ability to condition the generation process on additional information opens up many possibilities for creating more diverse and specific data.

Progressive Growing of GANs (ProGANs)

ProGANs is a machine learning technique used to generate images. The technique starts by generating low-resolution images and then increases the resolution gradually by adding new layers. This approach allows ProGANs to create more detailed and realistic images as compared to traditional GANs.

ProGANs were first introduced in a research paper titled "Progressive Growing of GANs for Improved Quality, Stability, and Variation" by Tero Karras, Timo Aila, Samuli Laine, and Jaakko Lehtinen. The paper explores the use of ProGANs to generate high-quality images of faces, landscapes, and other objects. ProGANs have since been used in various fields, including computer graphics, fashion, and gaming, to create realistic images and visual effects.

Wasserstein GANs (WGANs)

Generative Adversarial Networks (GANs) are a popular class of deep learning models that have shown impressive results in generating realistic images, videos, and audio. However, traditional GANs can be difficult to train due to their unstable training process. Wasserstein GANs (WGANs) are a modification of the original GAN architecture that uses a different loss function based on the Wasserstein distance.

This new loss function can provide better training stability and has shown promising results in generating high-quality images. In addition to their improved stability, WGANs are also known for their ability to enforce constraints on the generator's output distribution, which can be useful for certain applications.

StyleGANs

StyleGANs are a type of advanced GAN that are capable of generating high-quality images with unparalleled precision and control over the style of the generated images. They have revolutionized the field of image generation and have opened up a myriad of new possibilities, such as generating photorealistic images of objects and scenes that do not exist in the real world.

The technology behind StyleGANs is extremely complex and involves a deep understanding of both machine learning and computer graphics. However, their potential applications are limitless, and they are already being used in a variety of fields such as art, entertainment, and even medicine. With StyleGANs, the possibilities are endless, and it is exciting to think about the new frontiers that this technology will open up in the years to come.

Example:

Here's a simple example of how to modify our earlier code to make a conditional GAN:

```python
# Assuming we have a class label for each image
def train_step(images, labels):
    noise = tf.random.normal([BATCH_SIZE, 100])

    with tf.GradientTape() as gen_tape, tf.GradientTape() as disc_tape:
        generated_images = generator([noise, labels], training=True) # Pass labe
ls to the generator

        real_output = discriminator([images, labels], training=True) # Pass labe
ls to the discriminator
        fake_output = discriminator([generated_images, labels], training=True) #
Pass labels to the discriminator

        gen_loss = generator_loss(fake_output)
        disc_loss = discriminator_loss(real_output, fake_output)

    gradients_of_generator = gen_tape.gradient(gen_loss, generator.trainable_var
iables)
    gradients_of_discriminator = disc_tape.gradient(disc_loss, discriminator.tra
inable_variables)

    generator_optimizer.apply_gradients(zip(gradients_of_generator, generator.tr
ainable_variables))
    discriminator_optimizer.apply_gradients(zip(gradients_of_discriminator, disc
riminator.trainable_variables))
```

Code block 25

In this code, both the generator and the discriminator take an additional argument: the labels. The generator uses these labels to generate images that not only look real but also match the given class. The discriminator, in turn, is trained to classify not only the authenticity of the images but also their class.

These are just a few examples of the many ways in which the basic GAN architecture and training process can be modified and enhanced. Researchers continue to propose and test new ideas, so it's a good idea to stay up-to-date with the latest research if you're working with GANs.

3.4 Evaluating GANs

One of the main challenges when working with Generative Adversarial Networks (GANs) is assessing the quality of the generated samples. Unlike supervised learning tasks, we don't have a ground truth to compare the generated samples against, and so traditional metrics such as accuracy, precision, recall, or F1-score aren't applicable.

However, there are several methods that have been proposed to evaluate the performance of GANs. One such method involves using Inception Score, which measures the balance between the quality and diversity of generated samples. Another method is the Frechet Inception Distance (FID), which calculates the distance between the distribution of real and generated samples in a feature space.

Furthermore, researchers have been exploring alternative ways to evaluate GANs, such as through human evaluation or by considering the task-specific performance of the generated samples. By examining the strengths and limitations of these different methods, we can gain a better understanding of the evaluation challenges and opportunities in GAN research.

3.4.1 Visual Inspection

Evaluating the output of a GAN can be done in various ways. The most straightforward method is to visually inspect the generated images, as it allows for a quick and easy assessment of the quality and variety of the images produced. However, it is important to note that visual inspection can be highly subjective, and as such, it is not always the most accurate or reliable method of evaluation.

For a more quantitative measure that can be used to compare different models or training runs, other methods of evaluation may be necessary. One such method is to use a metric that measures image quality, such as Inception Score or Fréchet Inception Distance. These metrics can provide a more objective assessment of the quality and variety of images produced by the GAN.

It is also important to consider the scalability of the evaluation method used. Visual inspection, although effective for small datasets and low-resolution images, may not be practical for larger datasets or high-resolution images. In such cases, automated evaluation methods that are able to process large amounts of data quickly and accurately may be necessary.

While visual inspection is a simple and effective way to evaluate the output of a GAN, it is not always the most reliable or scalable method. Different evaluation methods may be required depending on the specific use case and requirements.

3.4.2 Inception Score

The Inception Score (IS) is a widely used metric for evaluating the effectiveness of Generative Adversarial Networks (GANs) to generate images. The IS is based on the assumption that good quality images should be both diverse, meaning that they should have a good variety of different images, and realistic, meaning that they should look like images from the training set.

To compute the Inception Score, you pass the generated images through the InceptionV3 model, which is a pre-trained image classification model. The model then outputs a probability distribution over the different classes of object that are present in the image. This distribution is then compared to the uniform distribution, and the Kullback-Leibler (KL) divergence between the two distributions is computed.

The KL divergence essentially measures the difference between the two distributions. If the two distributions are significantly different, then the KL divergence will be high, and this indicates that the generated images are not very diverse or realistic. On the other hand, if the two distributions are very similar, then the KL divergence will be low, and this indicates that the generated images are both diverse and realistic. Therefore, by computing the Inception Score, it's possible to determine how well the GAN is performing and whether it needs to be improved in order to generate better quality images.

Example:

Here's a simplified code snippet to compute the Inception Score:

```python
from tensorflow.keras.applications.inception_v3 import InceptionV3, preprocess_input

# Load pretrained InceptionV3 model
model = InceptionV3(include_top=True, weights='imagenet')

def compute_inception_score(images):
    # Preprocess images
    images = preprocess_input(images)

    # Compute predictions
    preds = model.predict(images)

    # Compute the inception score
    scores = np.exp(preds)
    scores /= np.sum(scores, axis=-1, keepdims=True)
    scores = np.log(scores) * scores
    scores = -np.sum(scores, axis=-1)
    inception_score = np.exp(np.mean(scores))

    return inception_score
```

Code block 26

3.4.3 Frechet Inception Distance

The Frechet Inception Distance (FID) is a widely used metric for evaluating the performance of GANs. One key difference between FID and the Inception Score is that FID considers both the generated and real images. This allows for a more comprehensive evaluation of the GAN's ability to generate images that are similar to real ones.

The FID metric computes the distance between the distributions of the generated and real images in the feature space of a pretrained model, which is usually InceptionV3. By considering both distributions, FID captures the degree to which the generated images match the real ones in terms of their features. This makes it a more robust metric for evaluating the quality of GAN-generated images.

Example:

Here's how you can compute the FID:

```python
from scipy.linalg import sqrtm

def compute_fid(images1, images2):
    # calculate mean and covariance statistics
    mu1, sigma1 = images1.mean(axis=0), np.cov(images1, rowvar=False)
    mu2, sigma2 = images2.mean(axis=0), np.cov(images2, rowvar=False)

    # calculate sum squared difference between means
    ssdiff = np.sum((mu1 - mu2)**2.0)

    # calculate sqrt of product between cov
    covmean = sqrtm(sigma1.dot(sigma2))

    # check and correct imaginary numbers from sqrt
    if np.iscomplexobj(covmean):
        covmean = covmean.real

    # calculate score
    fid = ssdiff + np.trace(sigma1 + sigma2 - 2.0 * covmean)
    return fid
```

Code block 27

These are just a few ways to quantitatively assess the performance of a GAN. It's important to remember that these metrics are not perfect and have their own limitations.

3.4.4 Precision, Recall, and F1 Score for GANs

Recent research has also proposed using concepts from information retrieval - specifically precision, recall, and F1 score - to evaluate GANs. These concepts have been found to be useful in determining the quality of the generated samples. In this context, precision measures how many of the generated samples are real (i.e., how many lie on the manifold of the training data), while recall measures how many of the real samples can be generated by the GAN.

However, determining what constitutes a "real" sample in high-dimensional space can be challenging. To address this issue, researchers have proposed using nearest-neighbor matching in the feature space of a pretrained model. This method involves finding the closest real sample to each generated sample in the feature space and then comparing their similarity. The generated samples with the highest similarity scores are considered the most "real".

Calculating these scores can be quite complex and involves multiple steps such as preprocessing the data, training the model, and conducting the nearest-neighbor matching. As such, it's beyond the scope of a beginner's book to cover these methods in detail. Nevertheless, it's good to be aware of these techniques and how they can be used to evaluate GANs more accurately.

3.4.5 Limitations of GAN Evaluation Metrics

While the above-mentioned metrics can provide quantitative measures of GAN performance, it is important to note that they have certain limitations. For example, both the Inception Score and FID rely on the InceptionV3 model, which was trained on the ImageNet dataset. However, if your GAN is generating images of a type not well-represented in ImageNet (e.g., medical images), relying solely on these scores may not be adequate.

To overcome this limitation, some researchers have proposed alternative methods such as Precision and Recall scores that can better capture the nuances of certain domains. However, it is important to note that these methods also have their own limitations and may not be perfect.

Furthermore, it is important to keep in mind that these metrics can sometimes contradict each other and human judgement. For instance, a model with a better (lower) FID score might produce images that humans judge to be of worse quality, or vice versa. Hence, there is no one-size-fits-all approach to evaluating GANs, and a more comprehensive and multidimensional approach, including human judgement and alternative evaluation metrics, is often the best way forward.

3.5 Variations of GANs

The generative adversarial network (GAN) framework has inspired many variations since its inception. These variations are designed to tackle different issues and shortcomings of the original GAN or to focus on different applications. In this section, we will discuss some of the most popular and influential variations of GANs.

3.5.1 Deep Convolutional GANs (DCGANs)

One of the earliest and most influential variations of GANs is the Deep Convolutional GAN (DCGAN). DCGANs were proposed as an extension of GANs where both the generator and discriminator are deep convolutional networks. They are known for their stability in training compared to vanilla GANs and are often a good starting point for those new to GANs.

Furthermore, DCGANs have been used in various applications such as image and video generation, style transfer, and data augmentation. The use of deep convolutional networks allows for more complex representations of the data, leading to higher quality and more realistic outputs.

One of the key contributions of DCGANs was a set of guidelines for constructing GANs such as using batch normalization, avoiding fully connected layers, and using certain activation functions. These principles have been widely adopted in the design of later GANs. In addition, researchers have extended the DCGAN architecture with various modifications such as incorporating attention mechanisms, using different loss functions, and introducing new network architectures. These developments have led to an expanding range of applications for GANs in fields such as computer vision, natural language processing, and even music generation.

External Reference: DCGAN on TensorFlow
(https://www.tensorflow.org/tutorials/generative/dcgan)

3.5.2 Conditional GANs (CGANs)

Conditional Generative Adversarial Networks (CGANs) are a powerful extension of Generative Adversarial Networks (GANs) that allow for the generation of data with specified characteristics. Compared to traditional GANs, CGANs introduce an additional input layer that is conditioned on some additional information, such as a class label or a set of attributes. This additional input layer is usually provided alongside the noise vector to the generator, and also alongside the real or generated sample to the discriminator. By leveraging this additional information, the model is able to generate data with specific attributes and characteristics, such as generating images of a particular type of clothing or a specific digit.

One of the key benefits of CGANs is their ability to generate data that is not only realistic, but also conforms to specific constraints or requirements. This makes them particularly useful in a variety of applications, from image generation to drug discovery and beyond. For instance, they can be used to generate synthetic images of people wearing specific types of clothing, which can be used to train machine learning models for tasks such as image recognition or object detection. Similarly, they can be used to generate synthetic molecules with specific properties, which can be used to accelerate the drug discovery process.

CGANs represent a major breakthrough in the field of generative modeling, offering researchers and practitioners alike a powerful tool for generating data with specific attributes and characteristics. By allowing the generator and discriminator to be conditioned on additional information, these models are able to learn more complex relationships between the input and output data, ultimately leading to more realistic and useful results.

External Reference: CGAN on Keras (https://keras.io/examples/generative/conditional_gan/)

3.5.3 Wasserstein GANs (WGANs)

Wasserstein Generative Adversarial Networks (WGANs) are a newer variation of the original GAN that have been designed to address some key challenges. One of the primary issues with the original GANs was that they tended to suffer from mode collapse, which limited their ability to generate diverse outputs. To address this issue, WGANs introduce a new way of measuring the difference between the generator's distribution and the real data distribution, using the Wasserstein distance (also known as the Earth Mover's distance). This approach has been shown to be more effective than the Jensen-Shannon divergence used in the original GAN.

In addition to addressing the mode collapse problem, WGANs also offer other advantages over traditional GANs. For example, they tend to be more stable during training, which can help to prevent the generator from producing poor quality outputs. They also offer more flexibility in terms of the types of architectures that can be used, making them a more versatile option for researchers and practitioners.

Despite these advantages, WGANs are not without their own limitations and challenges. For example, they can be more computationally expensive to train than traditional GANs, and may require more careful tuning of hyperparameters. However, overall, the use of Wasserstein distance and other modifications make WGANs a promising area of research for improving the performance and capabilities of generative models.

External Reference: WGAN on GitHub (https://github.com/eriklindernoren/Keras-GAN#wgan)

3.5.4 Progressive Growing of GANs (ProGANs)

ProGANs are a type of GAN, or generative adversarial network, that have been developed by NVIDIA. They differ from other GANs in that they start by training on low-resolution images and progressively increase the resolution by adding layers to the generator and discriminator during the training process. This unique approach makes the training process more stable and allows for the generation of high-quality, high-resolution images, which are becoming increasingly important in fields such as computer graphics and virtual reality.

By starting with low-resolution images, ProGANs are able to capture the basic features of an image before moving on to more complex details. This means that the generator is able to learn the underlying structure of an image before attempting to generate high-resolution versions of it. Additionally, the progressive approach means that the discriminator is able to learn at an appropriate pace, ensuring that the generator is not overwhelmed with too much information at once.

These capabilities have made ProGANs a popular choice among researchers and artists who are looking to create highly realistic synthetic images. Some of the most impressive examples of ProGAN-generated images include photorealistic landscapes, portraits, and even entire cityscapes. As computer technology continues to advance, it is likely that ProGANs will play an increasingly important role in the creation of high-quality, realistic images for a wide range of applications.

External Reference: ProGAN Official GitHub
(https://github.com/tkarras/progressive_growing_of_gans)

3.5.5 BigGANs and StyleGANs

BigGANs and StyleGANs are two types of GANs that have achieved state-of-the-art results in generating high-quality images. BigGANs are known for their large-scale and high-capacity models, which allow them to create images with a high level of detail and realism. They incorporate a range of techniques, such as spectral normalization and self-attention, that enable them to better capture the complex structure of real-world images.

StyleGANs, on the other hand, introduce a novel mechanism called style transfer to control the fine and coarse details of the generated images. This approach allows for greater control over the visual characteristics of the generated images, such as their color palette and texture. In addition, StyleGANs are able to generate images with a high degree of diversity, meaning that they are capable of producing a wide range of images with different visual styles and characteristics.

While BigGANs and StyleGANs are two of the most well-known and widely used types of GANs, there are many other variations of this model that have been developed in recent years. For example, CycleGANs are a type of GAN that can be used to perform image-to-image translation, allowing for the transfer of visual style and content between different images. Similarly, Progressive GANs are a type of GAN that can generate images at increasingly high resolutions, allowing for the creation of highly detailed and realistic images.

Each of these models extends the original GAN framework in interesting and innovative ways, and there is still much active research in this area. As researchers continue to develop new types of GANs and refine existing models, it is likely that we will see even more impressive results in the field of generative image modeling in the years to come.

External References:

BigGAN: BigGAN on TensorFlow Hub (https://tfhub.dev/deepmind/biggan-256/2)

StyleGAN: StyleGAN Official GitHub (https://github.com/NVlabs/stylegan)

In the next section, we will look at how these techniques are applied in practice by examining various use cases and applications of GANs.

3.6 Use Cases and Applications of GANs

Generative Adversarial Networks (GANs) have garnered significant attention in recent years due to their numerous powerful applications. These models can not only generate new content, but also enhance existing content, or discover and learn useful representations of input data. Given the vast range of potential applications of GANs, we will explore some of the exciting use cases and domains where they can be utilized.

One of the most popular applications of GANs is in the field of image generation and manipulation. By training a GAN on a dataset of images, it is possible to generate new images that look similar to the original dataset, but with unique characteristics. These generated images can be used in a variety of contexts, ranging from art to advertising.

Another interesting application of GANs is in the field of natural language processing (NLP). By training a GAN on a dataset of text, it is possible to generate new text that is similar in style and structure to the original dataset. This can be useful in a range of contexts, from chatbots to content creation.

GANs can also be used for data augmentation, which is particularly useful in applications such as computer vision. By using GANs to generate new images, it is possible to significantly increase the size of a dataset, which can improve the accuracy of machine learning models.

Due to the versatility and power of GANs, they have a wide range of potential applications in various domains. As such, they are an exciting area of research and development in the field of machine learning and artificial intelligence.

3.6.1 Image Synthesis

The ability of GANs to generate images that are strikingly similar to real photographs has been one of the most celebrated applications of these models. This has been made possible through the use of advanced machine learning algorithms that enable the creation of artificial photographs that look eerily similar to real images.

For instance, the website "This Person Does Not Exist" (https://this-person-does-not-exist.com/), which uses a variant of GAN known as StyleGAN, has been able to generate synthetic images of people that are so realistic that it is often difficult to tell whether they are real or not. This has opened up a new world of possibilities for artificial intelligence and computer graphics, as it allows for the creation of highly realistic images without the need for expensive photo shoots or painstaking manual labor.

3.6.2 Super-resolution

GANs, or Generative Adversarial Networks, have been found to have a multitude of uses in the field of image processing. One such application is in enhancing the resolution of images, which is commonly referred to as super-resolution. The process involves taking a low-resolution image as an input, and using a GAN to generate a higher resolution output. This process is made possible because the GAN is trained on high-resolution images, and is therefore able to add plausible details to the low-resolution input.

Super-resolution has a wide range of applications, making it a powerful tool for many industries. For example, in satellite imagery, super-resolution can be used to enhance the quality of images of the earth, which can aid in tasks such as predicting weather patterns, tracking natural disasters, and monitoring crop growth. In the field of medical imaging, super-resolution can be used to improve the quality of MRI and CT scans, which can help doctors make more accurate diagnoses. Finally, in video streaming, super-resolution can be used to improve the viewing experience of users by providing clearer and more detailed images.

External Resources:

For super-resolution, one of the prominent projects is the SRGAN (Super-Resolution Generative Adversarial Network). Here is the link to the SRGAN paper: **"Photo-Realistic Single Image Super-Resolution Using a Generative Adversarial Network"** (https://arxiv.org/abs/1609.04802).

Also, you can find an implementation of SRGAN on **GitHub** (https://github.com/deepak112/Keras-SRGAN).

Also, you can find an implementation of SRGAN on **GitHub** (.

3.6.3 Data Augmentation

Generative Adversarial Networks (GANs) are a powerful tool that can be used to augment datasets by generating synthetic data. This can be particularly useful in a variety of situations where collecting more real data is challenging or expensive. One example of where GANs can be especially helpful is in the field of healthcare. By using GANs to generate synthetic patient data, healthcare professionals can train other machine learning models without compromising patient privacy.

GANs can be used to simulate a wide range of scenarios, providing researchers with more data to work with. This could be especially beneficial in areas such as transportation or environmental studies, where it may be difficult or impossible to collect data in the real world. Overall, GANs have the potential to revolutionize the way we approach data analysis and machine learning, opening up new possibilities for researchers and practitioners alike.

External Resources:

For data augmentation, a good resource is this paper, **"Data Augmentation Generative Adversarial Networks"** (https://arxiv.org/abs/1711.04340), which explores using GANs for data augmentation.

3.6.4 Art and Design

Generative Adversarial Networks (GANs) have been used not only in the field of computer science but also in art and design. Their ability to generate new designs, patterns, or artwork can be an excellent source of inspiration for artists and designers alike. By using GANs, artists and designers can explore new creative possibilities and experiment with different styles and techniques.

GANs can help creators overcome creative blocks by providing them with starting points for their work. In this way, GANs have become a powerful tool in the creative process, allowing artists and designers to expand their creative horizons and push the boundaries of traditional art and design.

External Resources:

Artbreeder, as mentioned before, is a powerful tool for generating novel designs and artwork. Visit the **Artbreeder website** (https://www.artbreeder.com/) for more details.

3.6.5 Animation and Gaming

In the field of animation and game development, Generative Adversarial Networks (GANs) can be a powerful tool for creating new and unique visual assets. By training a GAN on a dataset of existing textures, character designs, and environmental elements, it can learn to generate new variations that fit within the same style and visual language. This not only reduces the amount of manual work required, but also adds diversity to the final product.

GANs can be used to create entirely new assets that may not have existed before, such as unique character designs or never-before-seen environmental elements. Overall, the use of GANs in animation and game development can greatly enhance the creative process and lead to more compelling and visually stunning projects.

External Resource:

GANPaint Studio is a project from MIT that uses GANs to enable intuitive, interactive painting of scenes, which could be of interest for gaming and animation. Here's the link to the **GANPaint Studio** (http://ganpaint.io/).

These are just a few examples of the exciting applications of GANs. As research progresses and these models continue to improve, we can expect even more innovative applications to emerge. The potential of GANs to contribute to various fields is immense and remains a hot area of research.

In the next chapter, we will dive into a practical project where we use GANs to generate synthetic faces. This will allow you to apply all the knowledge you've gained so far in a hands-on manner.

3.7 Practical Exercises

3.7.1 Implementing a Simple GAN

In this exercise, you will implement a simple GAN using Keras. Your task is to create both the generator and discriminator and then train them. You can use the MNIST dataset for this exercise.

```python
# Importing necessary libraries
from keras.datasets import mnist
from keras.layers import Input, Dense, Reshape, Flatten
from keras.layers import BatchNormalization
from keras.layers.advanced_activations import LeakyReLU
from keras.models import Sequential, Model
from keras.optimizers import Adam
import matplotlib.pyplot as plt
import numpy as np

# Set random seed for reproducibility
np.random.seed(1000)

# Load the dataset
(X_train, _), (_, _) = mnist.load_data()
X_train = (X_train.astype(np.float32) - 127.5) / 127.5
X_train = np.expand_dims(X_train, axis=3)

# Size of the noise vector, used as input to the Generator
z_dim = 100

# TODO: Implement the Generator and Discriminator here

# TODO: Define and compile the combined model here

# TODO: Train the GAN here
```

Code block 28

3.7.2 Implementing DCGAN

Next, you will implement a Deep Convolutional GAN (DCGAN). Similar to the previous exercise, your task is to create both the generator and discriminator and then train them. You can continue to use the MNIST dataset for this exercise.

```python
# Importing necessary libraries
from keras.datasets import mnist
from keras.layers import Input, Dense, Reshape, Flatten, Conv2D, Conv2DTranspose
from keras.layers import BatchNormalization
from keras.layers.advanced_activations import LeakyReLU
from keras.models import Sequential, Model
from keras.optimizers import Adam
import matplotlib.pyplot as plt
import numpy as np

# Set random seed for reproducibility
np.random.seed(1000)

# Load the dataset
(X_train, _), (_, _) = mnist.load_data()
X_train = (X_train.astype(np.float32) - 127.5) / 127.5
X_train = np.expand_dims(X_train, axis=3)

# Size of the noise vector, used as input to the Generator
z_dim = 100

# TODO: Implement the Generator and Discriminator for DCGAN here

# TODO: Define and compile the combined model here

# TODO: Train the DCGAN here
```

Code block 29

Remember, these exercises are starting points for you to experiment. You can tweak the architecture, change the optimizer, or use a different dataset to see how these changes impact the GAN's performance. Be sure to try out different configurations and see what works best!

Chapter 3 Conclusion

In this chapter, we delved deep into the realm of Generative Adversarial Networks (GANs), starting with their basic understanding and gradually expanding into their intricate architecture, training process, various modifications, and potential applications.

We began by grasping the conceptual underpinnings of GANs and how they revolutionize generative modeling by embodying a unique adversarial relationship between the generator and discriminator.

This concept was further elaborated as we explored the architecture of GANs, unveiling the functionalities and intricacies of both the generator and discriminator networks.

As we ventured into the training process of GANs, we navigated the challenges of training stability, mode collapse, and the delicate balance that needs to be maintained to ensure effective learning. These challenges hint at the intricacy and nuanced nature of GANs, which further diversify with the emergence of various GAN variants.

From the foundational GAN structure, many creative and practical variations have emerged, each having its own merits and suited use cases. We briefly touched upon some of these variations, such as DCGAN, WGAN, and cGAN, each extending the scope and capability of the original GAN model.

Then we turned our attention to the exciting part of the potential applications of GANs. From generating realistic human faces to enhancing image resolution, augmenting data, generating art, and even influencing the fields of animation and gaming, GANs are painting a future with limitless possibilities.

Finally, we concluded with some practical exercises for you to get your hands dirty. This will provide a real sense of the GAN structure and how to implement and train them using Keras.

In the next chapter, we will focus on one of the most popular applications of GANs, which is generating new faces. The project-based approach will enable you to apply the theoretical knowledge you've acquired so far and gain practical experience in developing a GAN project from scratch. So, let's gear up and dive into the next chapter!

Stay curious, keep learning, and remember - with GANs, you're limited only by your imagination!

Chapter 4: Project: Face Generation with GANs

Welcome to Chapter 4, where we put theory into practice by taking on a project on face generation with GANs. Having covered the theory behind GANs in detail in the previous chapter, this project-based chapter will help solidify your understanding of how to implement and use GANs for real-world applications.

Our main aim in this project is to develop a GAN model that can generate realistic human faces. This involves the entire workflow of a typical machine learning project, starting with data collection and preprocessing, through model development, training, and finally evaluation of the results. Throughout the chapter, we will provide code examples and explain each step in the process in detail.

Let's begin with the first step: Data Collection and Preprocessing.

4.1 Data Collection and Preprocessing

Data is the lifeblood of machine learning models. Good data leads to good models. When it comes to generative models like GANs, we need a substantial amount of data to learn the underlying distribution. For our face generation project, we require a dataset of human faces.

One popular dataset for this purpose is the **CelebA** dataset (http://mmlab.ie.cuhk.edu.hk/projects/CelebA.html). It contains over 200,000 celebrity images centered on the face and reasonably uniform. This publicly available dataset has been widely used in many face-related machine learning projects.

To download and use the CelebA dataset in our project, we can use the code snippet below:

```
# Note: The actual download link might be different. Please refer to the officia
l CelebA website.
!wget https://mmlab.ie.cuhk.edu.hk/projects/CelebA/Dataset/CelebA.zip
!unzip CelebA.zip
```

Code block 30

Once we have the dataset, the next step is preprocessing. Preprocessing involves getting the data into a suitable format that can be fed into our GAN. This might involve resizing images, normalizing pixel values, etc. For our project, we will resize all images to 64x64 and normalize the pixel values to be in the range [-1, 1]. The preprocessing can be done using the following code:

```python
from PIL import Image
import os
import numpy as np

def preprocess_images(image_path):
    """
    Function to preprocess images: resize and normalize
    """
    # Load image
    img = Image.open(image_path)

    # Resize to 64x64
    img = img.resize((64, 64))

    # Convert to numpy array and normalize
    img_array = np.array(img)
    img_array = img_array / 127.5 - 1

    return img_array

# Path to CelebA dataset
dataset_path = "/path/to/CelebA/dataset"

# Get list of all images
image_paths = os.listdir(dataset_path)

# Preprocess all images
images = [preprocess_images(os.path.join(dataset_path, img_path)) for img_path i
n image_paths]
```

Code block 31

After executing the above code, we have a list of preprocessed images ready to be used for training our GAN. In the next section, we will discuss how to create a GAN for our face generation task.

NOTE: Remember that using datasets like CelebA requires adherence to their usage terms and conditions, especially regarding privacy and ethical considerations.

4.1.1 Dataset Splitting

Before we move on to creating our GAN model, we need to split our data into a training set and a validation set. The training set is used to train the model, while the validation set is used to evaluate the model's performance on unseen data during the training process. This helps us monitor if the model is overfitting to the training data.

In most cases, we split the data into 80% training and 20% validation. However, because GANs typically do not use a validation set in the traditional sense (since they do not need labelled data), we will use all the data for training in this case.

This is a deviation from the usual practice, but remember that GANs are generative models and the concept of "overfitting" can be a bit different here compared to discriminative models (like a standard neural network). The idea is to make the GAN learn the data distribution as best as it can.

So, although we are not doing a traditional train-validation split here, understanding the concept is important for most other machine learning models. In such cases, the split can be easily achieved using scikit-learn's **train_test_split** function, as shown in the example code snippet below:

```python
from sklearn.model_selection import train_test_split

# Convert list of images to numpy array
images = np.array(images)

# Split the data into training and validation sets
# (not applicable for GANs, but good to know for general ML models)
# train_images, val_images = train_test_split(images, test_size=0.2, random_stat
e=42)
```

Code block 32

With the data collection, preprocessing, and understanding of dataset splitting complete, we're ready to dive into the next step: creating our GAN model!

Please remember that the above code of splitting the dataset into training and validation is not necessary for GANs, but it's crucial to understand this process as it's a standard procedure in many other machine learning projects.

4.2 Model Creation

The model creation stage involves defining the architecture of our Generative Adversarial Network (GAN). As we know from Chapter 3, a GAN is composed of two main parts: the generator and the discriminator.

4.2.1 The Generator

The generator's purpose is to generate new data from random noise. The output of the generator should ideally be indistinguishable from the true data.

In our case, we're generating images, so our generator will output an image of the same size as the training images.

We'll use a Deep Convolutional GAN (DCGAN) structure for our generator. Here is an example of what the generator's architecture might look like in code:

```python
from keras.models import Sequential
from keras.layers import Dense, Reshape, Conv2DTranspose, LeakyReLU, BatchNormal
ization

# Generator model
def create_generator(latent_dim):
    model = Sequential()

    # Start with dense layer from which to reshape
    model.add(Dense(256*16*16, input_dim=latent_dim))
    model.add(LeakyReLU(alpha=0.2))
    model.add(Reshape((16, 16, 256)))

    # Up-sample to 32x32
    model.add(Conv2DTranspose(128, (4,4), strides=(2,2), padding='same'))
    model.add(LeakyReLU(alpha=0.2))
    model.add(BatchNormalization(momentum=0.8))

    # Up-sample to 64x64
    model.add(Conv2DTranspose(64, (4,4), strides=(2,2), padding='same'))
    model.add(LeakyReLU(alpha=0.2))
    model.add(BatchNormalization(momentum=0.8))

    # Output layer
    model.add(Conv2DTranspose(3, (3,3), activation='tanh', padding='same'))

    return model
```

Code block 33

This model starts with a dense layer and reshapes it into a multi-dimensional tensor. It then uses convolutional transpose layers (also known as deconvolutional layers) to upsample the data and generate an image.

4.2.2 The Discriminator

The discriminator's job is to distinguish between the real and fake (generated) images. It's essentially a binary classification model that classifies images as real (1) or fake (0).

Like our generator, we'll use a convolutional structure for our discriminator. Here's an example of what the discriminator's architecture might look like:

```python
from keras.layers import Conv2D, Flatten, Dropout

# Discriminator model
def create_discriminator(image_shape):
    model = Sequential()

    # Down-sample to 32x32
    model.add(Conv2D(64, (3,3), strides=(2,2), padding='same', input_shape=image
_shape))
    model.add(LeakyReLU(alpha=0.2))

    # Down-sample to 16x16
    model.add(Conv2D(128, (3,3), strides=(2,2), padding='same'))
    model.add(LeakyReLU(alpha=0.2))
    model.add(Dropout(0.4))

    # Down-sample to 8x8
    model.add(Conv2D(256, (3,3), strides=(2,2), padding='same'))
    model.add(LeakyReLU(alpha=0.2))
    model.add(Dropout(0.4))

    # Classifier
    model.add(Flatten())
    model.add(Dense(1, activation='sigmoid'))

    return model
```

Code block 34

This model uses standard convolutional layers to downsample the input image and classify it as real or fake. The dropout layers are used to prevent overfitting, and the LeakyReLU activation function is used to introduce nonlinearity into the model.

These code snippets provided here are a good starting point for the architecture of the GAN. However, when it comes to designing your own GAN for a specific task, a lot of experimentation is often needed to find an architecture and set of hyperparameters that work well.

With the generator and discriminator defined, we can now compile them into a GAN. The GAN will chain the generator and discriminator together: the generator will receive a point from the latent space as input and will output a candidate image, which will be fed into the discriminator alongside real images.

Here's an example of how we can compile our models into a GAN:

```python
from keras.models import Model
from keras.optimizers import Adam

# Build and compile the discriminator
discriminator = create_discriminator(image_shape)
discriminator.compile(loss='binary_crossentropy',
                      optimizer=Adam(0.0002, 0.5),
                      metrics=['accuracy'])

# Build the generator
generator = create_generator(latent_dim)

# The generator takes noise as input and generates imgs
z = Input(shape=(latent_dim,))
img = generator(z)

# For the combined model we will only train the generator
discriminator.trainable = False

# The discriminator takes generated images as input and determines validity
validity = discriminator(img)

# The combined model  (stacked generator and discriminator)
# Trains the generator to fool the discriminator
combined = Model(z, validity)
combined.compile(loss='binary_crossentropy',
                 optimizer=Adam(0.0002, 0.5))
```

Code block 35

This sets up the basic model structure for our GAN. The generator and discriminator are trained in tandem: the discriminator learning to better distinguish real from fake, and the generator learning to create more convincing fakes based on the discriminator's feedback.

In the next sections, we will look at how to train this model and generate new faces.

4.3 Training the GAN

Training a GAN involves simultaneously training the generator to produce more realistic images and training the discriminator to become better at distinguishing generated images from real ones. This is typically done in alternating phases: first, the discriminator is trained for one or more epochs, then the generator is trained for a number of epochs.

To train the discriminator, we'll feed it batches of real images labeled as real (1) and generated images labeled as fake (0), and update its weights based on how well it classified the images.

To train the generator, we'll use the combined model, which chains the generator to the discriminator. The combined model is trained using random noise labeled as real (1). Because the discriminator is frozen during the generator's training phase (i.e., **discriminator.trainable = False**), only the generator's weights are updated. The generator's training objective is to get the discriminator to classify its generated images as real.

Here's the training loop in Python, using Keras:

```python
import numpy as np

def train(GAN, generator, discriminator, dataset, latent_dim, n_epochs=5000, n_b
atch=128):
    half_batch = int(n_batch / 2)
    # manually enumerate epochs
    for i in range(n_epochs):
        # prepare real samples
        x_real, y_real = generate_real_samples(dataset, half_batch)
        # prepare fake examples
        x_fake, y_fake = generate_fake_samples(generator, latent_dim, half_batc
h)
        # update discriminator
        discriminator.train_on_batch(x_real, y_real)
        discriminator.train_on_batch(x_fake, y_fake)
        # prepare points in latent space as input for the generator
        x_gan = generate_latent_points(latent_dim, n_batch)
        # create inverted labels for the fake samples
        y_gan = np.ones((n_batch, 1))
        # update the generator via the discriminator's error
        GAN.train_on_batch(x_gan, y_gan)
        # evaluate the model every n_eval epochs
        if (i+1) % 500 == 0:
            summarize_performance(i, generator, discriminator, dataset, latent_d
im)
```

Code block 36

In this code, **generate_real_samples()** and **generate_fake_samples()** are functions that generate a batch of real and fake images, respectively, with appropriate labels, and **summarize_performance()** is a function that evaluates the discriminator's performance and saves the generator's output at different points during training. The specific implementation of these functions will depend on your dataset and the specific requirements of your project.

This process is repeated for a number of epochs until the generator and discriminator are both trained to a satisfactory level. The generator will hopefully produce convincing images, while the discriminator should be able to accurately distinguish between real and fake images.

In the next section, we'll take a look at how to generate new faces using our trained GAN.

4.4 Generating New Faces

Now that we have trained our GAN, we can use it to generate new images! In this section, we'll show how to generate images from our trained GAN, and then we'll discuss how to interpret and evaluate the results.

4.4.1 Generating Images from the GAN

To generate images from the GAN, we need to use the generator network. The generator has been trained to transform noise vectors (randomly generated inputs) into images, so all we need to do is to generate some noise and pass it through the generator.

Here is how we can do it in Python, using TensorFlow:

```python
def generate_images(generator, num_images):
    # We generate num_images random noise vectors
    noise = tf.random.normal([num_images, noise_dim])

    # We use the generator to transform the noise into images
    generated_images = generator(noise, training=False)

    # The generator outputs images in the range [-1, 1], so we rescale them to
[0, 1]
    generated_images = (generated_images + 1) / 2.0

    return generated_images.numpy()

# We generate 10 images and plot them
generated_images = generate_images(generator, 10)
for i in range(10):
    plt.subplot(2, 5, i+1)
    plt.imshow(generated_images[i])
    plt.axis('off')
plt.show()
```

Code block 37

This will create a plot with 10 images generated by our GAN. These images are entirely new faces, created by the GAN based on its training on the CelebA dataset.

4.4.2 Evaluating the Generated Images

The quality of the generated images is subjective and can be somewhat difficult to evaluate. When looking at the generated images, here are a few things that you might want to consider:

- **Diversity**: Are all the faces the GAN generates looking too similar, or is there a good variety in the generated images? If all images look too similar, this might be a sign of mode collapse, a common problem in training GANs.
- **Realism**: Do the generated images look like real faces? Are there any common artifacts or mistakes?
- **Detail**: Does the GAN capture small details correctly, like the texture of the hair or the reflections in the eyes?

Remember that GANs are a form of unsupervised learning, so they might capture and exaggerate patterns in the data that we humans don't pay much attention to. This is part of what makes working with GANs so fascinating: they can surprise us and show us a new perspective on the data!

4.4.3 Post-processing and Usage

Generated images can be used directly in a variety of applications, from art to advertising. Alternatively, they can be further processed or combined with other images. The specific post-processing steps will depend on your application.

As you can see, with GANs, we have a powerful tool for generating new data. However, like any powerful tool, GANs should be used responsibly. As we discussed in the previous chapter, GANs can also be used for malicious purposes, like creating deepfakes. It's essential to be mindful of the ethical implications of the technologies we create and use.

In the next section, we will wrap up this project and discuss some potential extensions and future directions.

4.5 Advanced Topics

4.5.1 Understanding Mode Collapse

Mode collapse is a common issue in GANs where the generator starts producing similar outputs for different inputs, effectively collapsing all the different modes of the data distribution into one. This is typically due to the generator finding a particular output that can fool the discriminator and sticking with it. This reduces the diversity of the generated samples.

One of the techniques used to combat mode collapse is to implement a variety of GAN architecture called Wasserstein GAN (WGAN). It modifies the GAN loss function to use the Wasserstein distance, which gives smoother gradients and makes it easier for the GAN to learn. Other methods include minibatch discrimination, unrolled GANs, or pacGANs.

4.5.2 Advanced Techniques for Evaluating GANs

While we've discussed some basic techniques to visually assess the quality of the generated faces, in practice, researchers often use more quantitative metrics. The Inception Score (IS) and the Frechet Inception Distance (FID) are among the most popular.

The Inception Score utilizes a pre-trained model (usually the Inception model, hence the name) to evaluate the quality and diversity of the generated images. However, IS has several shortcomings, so researchers developed the Frechet Inception Distance. FID also uses a pre-trained model to capture the feature distribution of real and generated images and measures the distance between these distributions, providing a more reliable evaluation.

However, these metrics require a pre-trained model and can be computationally expensive. They also don't necessarily correlate perfectly with human judgment of image quality, so visual assessment still plays a crucial role.

4.5.3 Tips for Improving Image Quality

There are several strategies to improve the quality of the generated images. Using deeper architectures, for instance, often leads to better results. The DCGAN paper recommends using strided convolutions for downsampling, fractional-strided convolutions for upsampling, and batch normalization in both the generator and the discriminator.

Adding noise to the inputs of the discriminator, a technique called instance noise, can stabilize GAN training and improve the quality of the outputs. Gradient penalty methods, like the one used in WGAN-GP, can also improve training stability.

More recently, researchers have been exploring self-attention mechanisms, introduced in the SAGAN paper, to allow the models to capture long-range dependencies in the images, which can lead to more coherent and high-quality outputs.

Now that we've explored these advanced topics, we can move on to the final step of our project in the next topic: 4.5 Evaluation and Conclusion.

4.6 Evaluation and Conclusion

At this point, you should have a working model that generates new human faces after being trained on a dataset of celebrity faces. The model architecture, parameters, and training procedure were explained in the previous sections, and hopefully, the project was a learning experience.

It's essential to evaluate the work done, reflecting on the success and limitations of the model and identifying potential areas for improvement.

4.6.1 Qualitative Evaluation

Evaluating GANs, especially in a project like this, involves a considerable qualitative component.

Take a moment to visually inspect the images your model is generating. Are they recognizable as human faces? Do they show a diverse range of features, or are they all quite similar? These are some of the questions that can guide your qualitative evaluation. Remember, in generative models, the goal isn't to reproduce the training data but to learn its distribution so the model can generate diverse, novel outputs that still lie within the learned distribution.

```python
# Generate a batch of new faces
generated_faces = generator.predict(noise)

# Visualize generated faces
for i in range(6):
    plt.subplot(2, 3, i+1)
    plt.imshow(generated_faces[i, :, :, 0], cmap='gray')
    plt.axis('off')
plt.show()
```

Code block 38

4.6.2 Quantitative Evaluation

Quantitative evaluation is a bit trickier for generative models like GANs. We've touched upon a couple of advanced techniques in Section 4.5.2, but it's beyond this project's scope to fully implement them. For now, we can only suggest that interested readers explore these avenues in more depth. The FID (Fréchet Inception Distance) or Inception Score might be beneficial for those who wish to dive deeper into evaluating GANs.

4.6.3 Reflection and Future Work

Reflect on the process of building this GAN. Which parts were the most challenging? Which parts were the most interesting? Do you feel like you understand GANs better now that you've worked through this project?

GANs are a powerful tool, but like any tool, they can be improved. Consider how you might refine this face-generating GAN further. Could the model architecture be tweaked for better results? Would more training data improve the output, or perhaps a more diverse set of faces? Could you apply some of the techniques and models discussed in Section 3.5?

Lastly, consider how you might adapt this GAN for other projects. The principles of GANs apply across different domains. With some modifications to the data and potentially to the model architecture, you could build a GAN that generates pictures of animals, handwritten digits, or even landscapes. The possibilities are endless, so don't stop exploring!

I hope you enjoyed this project as much as we enjoyed guiding you through it. Keep learning, keep building, and, most importantly, keep having fun while you're doing it!

4.7 Example of Full Code for the Project

In this section, you will get a high-level template demonstrating the key components of the GAN and how they fit together. However, it lacks some specific implementation details. For example, the **forward** functions of the Generator and Discriminator, the training steps within the training loop, and the specifics of the data preprocessing step are not included.

These parts are highly dependent on the specific architecture of your GAN and the dataset you're working with. They're also the parts of the code where you'd do the majority of your experimenting and fine-tuning, so they're less amenable to being included in a template. These are the details that were covered in the different sections of this chapter.

```python
# Required Libraries
import torch
from torch import nn
from torchvision import transforms, datasets
import matplotlib.pyplot as plt
import numpy as np

# Load and preprocess the data
transform = transforms.Compose([transforms.ToTensor(),
                                transforms.Normalize((0.5, 0.5, 0.5), (0.5, 0.5,
0.5))])
dataset = datasets.CelebA(root='./data', download=True, transform=transform)
dataloader = torch.utils.data.DataLoader(dataset, batch_size=64, shuffle=True)

# Define the Generator
class Generator(nn.Module):
    def __init__(self, z_size, conv_dim):
        super(Generator, self).__init__()
        # complete init function
    def forward(self, x):
        # complete forward function

# Define the Discriminator
class Discriminator(nn.Module):
    def __init__(self, conv_dim):
        super(Discriminator, self).__init__()
        # complete init function
    def forward(self, x):
        # complete forward function

# Training parameters
z_size = 100
conv_dim = 32
```

```python
G = Generator(z_size=z_size, conv_dim=conv_dim)
D = Discriminator(conv_dim=conv_dim)

# Define loss
criterion = nn.BCEWithLogitsLoss()

# Optimizers
lr = 0.0002
beta1=0.5
beta2=0.999

g_optimizer = torch.optim.Adam(G.parameters(), lr, [beta1, beta2])
d_optimizer = torch.optim.Adam(D.parameters(), lr, [beta1, beta2])

# Training
num_epochs = 30

for epoch in range(num_epochs):
    for real_images, _ in dataloader:
        # Training the Discriminator
        # your code here

        # Training the Generator
        # your code here

# Generate new faces
with torch.no_grad():
    z = torch.randn(64, z_size).to(device)
    generated_faces = G(z)
```

Code block 39

Note: Remember, this code is not complete. It only serves as a template to indicate how the code for the entire project could look. The complete code would contain full definitions of the Generator and Discriminator classes, the training code within the for loops, data preprocessing steps, as well as other necessary components for the project. For brevity, those sections are not included here. The full detailed code should follow the step-by-step guidelines discussed in each section of the chapter.

Chapter 4 Conclusion

Congratulations on completing your first project using Generative Adversarial Networks (GANs)! In this chapter, we've covered every step of creating a GAN from start to finish. We've gone through the process of collecting and preprocessing data, constructing the Generator and Discriminator components of the GAN, training the GAN, and using it to generate new faces.

We've also dived deeper into some advanced topics like improving the quality of generated images, making the training process more stable, and extending our GAN with conditional inputs. We have seen how GANs, despite their complexity, can be understood, implemented, and modified when broken down into their individual components.

The project we undertook was a challenging one: generating realistic human faces. This task is a testament to the power of GANs and their impact on the field of generative deep learning. Our project demonstrated how this complex task can be accomplished with a well-designed and well-trained GAN.

Remember that the process doesn't stop here. GANs are a deep and complex subject, and there is always more to learn and experiment with. This project should serve as a solid foundation, but don't be afraid to venture into more complex architectures, different types of data, and new ideas. The field is rapidly evolving, and there's always something new and exciting to discover.

In the next chapter, we'll explore another important category of generative models: Variational Autoencoders (VAEs). Like GANs, they provide a powerful way to generate new data, but they approach the problem from a different angle and offer their own unique advantages.

Onward to the next step in your generative deep learning journey!

Chapter 5: Exploring Variational Autoencoders (VAEs)

Welcome to Chapter 5 of our journey, where we delve deep into the world of Variational Autoencoders (VAEs). After exploring Generative Adversarial Networks (GANs) and experiencing their potential firsthand in the previous chapter, we now turn our attention to another revolutionary generative model that has contributed significantly to the advancement of machine learning and AI.

Variational Autoencoders, or VAEs, have become increasingly popular in recent years due to their ability to provide a probabilistic manner for describing an observation in latent space, which in turn has led to a wide range of applications in various fields such as image and speech recognition, natural language processing, and more. VAEs are considered to be more statistically rigorous than GANs, and yet, they can be trained with standard backpropagation techniques. The learning and understanding of VAEs is an essential part of anyone's journey who seeks to explore the depths of generative models.

In this chapter, we'll start by understanding the principles behind VAEs, including their theoretical underpinnings, and explore how they differ from other generative models such as GANs. We'll then delve into the architecture of VAEs, including the encoder and decoder networks, and examine how they work together to achieve the desired output. Next, we'll discuss the training process for VAEs, including the loss function and optimization techniques. Finally, we'll get our hands dirty with coding, where we will build, train, and test a VAE of our own, giving you the hands-on experience you need to truly understand these powerful generative models. So buckle up and get ready to explore the fascinating world of VAEs with us!

5.1 Understanding Variational Autoencoders (VAEs)

A Variational Autoencoder (VAE) is a type of neural network that is used to map inputs, such as images, to a set of latent variables. The latent variables are essentially a compressed representation of the input data that can be modified to generate new outputs. The idea behind a VAE is to learn a probability distribution over the latent variables that can be used to generate new data that is similar to the input data.

To achieve this, VAEs use a particular type of autoencoder that is capable of learning the underlying probability distribution over the input data. The encoder part of the VAE converts the input data into a compressed latent representation, while the decoder part reconstructs the input data from the compressed latent representation. The key idea behind a VAE is to learn a probability distribution over the latent variables that can be used to generate new outputs that are similar to the input data.

Variational inference is used to learn the probability distribution over the latent variables. This involves using a variational lower bound to estimate the likelihood of the data given the latent variables. The lower bound is optimized using stochastic gradient descent, which allows the VAE to learn the underlying probability distribution over the latent variables.

VAEs are a powerful tool for generating new data that is similar to the input data. They work by learning a probability distribution over a compressed latent representation of the input data that can be used to generate new outputs. The key idea behind VAEs is to use variational inference to learn the underlying probability distribution over the latent variables.

5.1.1 What is Variational Inference?

Variational inference is a powerful method used in Bayesian machine learning that allows for the expression of complex distributions in terms of simpler ones. In doing so, it provides a way to estimate intractable probability distributions. One of the key advantages of variational inference is that it allows for more efficient computation than other methods.

This is because instead of sampling directly from a distribution, it transforms the problem into an optimization problem, which can be solved using various techniques such as gradient descent. Additionally, variational inference has been shown to be effective in a wide range of applications including natural language processing and computer vision.

For example, it has been used to model text data and to perform image classification tasks. Overall, variational inference is an important tool for any practitioner working in the field of machine learning, and its applications continue to expand and grow in importance.

Here's a very simplified view of what a VAE does:

```
# Encoding
z_mean, z_log_variance = encoder(input_data)

# Sampling from the distribution
z = z_mean + exp(z_log_variance) * epsilon

# Decoding
reconstructed_data = decoder(z)
```

Code block 40

In this code:

- The **encoder** function takes the **input_data** and encodes it into two parameters in a latent space of representations, **z_mean** and **z_log_variance**.
- **epsilon** is a random tensor of small values. The random part is crucial: it ensures that every point that is close to the location where we encoded **input_data** can be decoded to something similar to **input_data**, thus enforcing the continuity of the latent space (and therefore the compactness). The parameters of the distribution are entirely learned from the data.
- The **decoder** function maps these sampled latent points back to the original input data.

During training, the parameters of the encoder, the decoder, and the sampler are learned simultaneously. This is achieved through a series of complex mathematical computations that are designed to optimize the performance of the model. In order to accomplish this, the model is trained on a large dataset that contains a wide variety of examples and scenarios.

The training process is iterative, with the model being adjusted and refined after each iteration. Through this process, the model gradually becomes more accurate and better able to handle the complexities of the task. Finally, once the training process is complete, the model can be used to generate new data or to make predictions based on existing data.

5.1.2 Latent Space and Its Significance

The concept of latent space is central to understanding VAEs. The "latent" variables in the latent space represent the fundamental structure and characteristics of the data. You can think of these variables as a compressed representation of the data that maintains the most crucial aspects.

In the context of VAEs, the latent variables are the learned parameters (mean and variance) that define the distributions from which we sample to generate new data. They capture the statistical properties of the data.

An important aspect of this latent space is that it should be "continuous", which is a desirable property for many tasks. Continuity means that small changes in the latent variables result in minor changes in the generated output. For instance, if we're dealing with images of faces, a smooth transition in the latent space should correspond to a smooth transition in the variations of the faces, like changing facial expressions or the angle of the face.

VAEs, by design, enforce a smooth, continuous latent space. This property makes them an excellent choice for many tasks that require the generation of new, realistic data samples.

Lastly, I think it's essential to highlight a unique aspect of VAEs: their roots in Bayesian Inference. VAEs belong to the family of techniques known as Bayesian deep learning, which combines the strengths of Bayesian probability theory and deep learning. Bayesian methods provide a framework for reasoning about uncertainty in the model parameters, which is an important consideration when we're learning representations in an unsupervised manner.

In summary, the magic of VAEs is in how they combine these principles - deep learning, Bayesian inference, and the concept of a smooth latent space - to provide a powerful framework for learning representations and generating new data.

Example:

Once we have a trained VAE, we can visualize the latent space to gain some insights. The details of this process vary depending on the specific type of data you're working with. Here is a general sketch of how this might look like in Python using matplotlib for visualization:

```python
# Assume vae_model is our trained VAE model
# Assume x_test is our test dataset

# Encode the data to get the latent variables
# Note: in practice, the encoder output is often a distribution parameters from
which we sample the latent variables
latent_variables = vae_model.encoder(x_test)

# We will only visualize the first 2 dimensions of the latent variables for simp
licity
latent_variables = latent_variables[:, :2]

# Plot the latent space
plt.scatter(latent_variables[:, 0], latent_variables[:, 1])
plt.xlabel('Latent variable 1')
plt.ylabel('Latent variable 2')
plt.title('Visualization of the latent space')
plt.show()
```

Code block 41

This is a simplistic visualization and might not be very meaningful if the latent space has more than 2 dimensions (which is typically the case). However, techniques such as t-SNE can be used to reduce the dimensionality of the latent space for a more meaningful visualization.

Please note that the actual code to visualize the latent space can vary greatly depending on the specifics of your VAE model and data. This is just a general template to give you an idea of how to approach this task.

In the later sections of this chapter, as we delve deeper into the details of building and training a VAE, we will have more concrete and detailed code examples.

5.2 Architecture of Variational Autoencoders (VAEs)

The Variational Autoencoder (VAE) is a type of artificial neural network that has been gaining popularity in recent years due to its unique architecture, which sets it apart from traditional autoencoders. While traditional autoencoders consist of an encoder that maps the input to a hidden representation and a decoder that reconstructs the input from the hidden representation, VAEs have an additional layer in the middle that learns the distribution of the data in the latent space. This middle layer is known as the "bottleneck" layer.

One of the key advantages of VAEs is that they allow for the generation of new data points that are similar to the original data. This is achieved by sampling from the learned distribution in the bottleneck layer. Additionally, VAEs are able to learn a more compressed representation of the data than traditional autoencoders. This is because the bottleneck layer is constrained to learn a distribution of the data, which forces it to capture the most salient features of the input.

The VAE is a powerful tool for data generation and compression due to its unique architecture that incorporates a bottleneck layer that learns the distribution of the data in the latent space.

5.2.1 Encoder Network

The Encoder or Recognition network is a crucial part of the Variational Autoencoder (VAE) architecture, which is often implemented using a convolutional neural network (CNN) or a fully connected network. Its main function is to take in the input data and compress it into a lower-dimensional representation. However, unlike a typical autoencoder that directly encodes input data into a fixed vector, the VAE's encoder outputs parameters of a probability distribution.

These parameters typically represent the mean and variance of a Gaussian distribution. By using this strategy, the VAE introduces randomness into the system, which can aid in generating new samples later on. This randomness helps the VAE to explore the latent space of the data, which can lead to more interesting and diverse outputs. By doing so, the VAE can learn more about the underlying structure of the data, and better capture its key features.

Example:

Let's look at an example. Here we have a simple VAE with an encoder network comprising a single fully connected hidden layer. The input dimension is **784** (for MNIST images), and the latent space dimension is **2**.

```python
class Encoder(nn.Module):
    def __init__(self, input_dim, hidden_dim, z_dim):
        super().__init__()

        self.linear = nn.Linear(input_dim, hidden_dim)
        self.mu = nn.Linear(hidden_dim, z_dim)
        self.var = nn.Linear(hidden_dim, z_dim)

    def forward(self, x):
        hidden = F.relu(self.linear(x))
        z_mu = self.mu(hidden)
        z_var = self.var(hidden)

        return z_mu, z_var
```

Code block 42

In this code snippet, **input_dim** refers to the size of the input data, **hidden_dim** is the size of the hidden layer, and **z_dim** is the dimension of the latent space. The **forward** function first applies a linear transformation and a ReLU activation to the input. It then computes **z_mu** (mean) and **z_var** (variance) using two separate linear transformations.

5.2.2 Reparameterization Trick

The reparameterization trick is a useful technique in deep learning that allows us to apply backpropagation to our network. This technique comes in handy when we need to sample from the distribution defined by the mean and variance. Instead of relying on the standard method to sample directly from this distribution, we use the reparameterization trick to first sample from a unit Gaussian distribution, and then we shift the resulting sample by the mean and scale it by the standard deviation.

This trick has several advantages over the direct sampling method. Firstly, it ensures that the gradients are well-defined, which is essential for backpropagation. Secondly, it allows us to compute the gradients with respect to the mean and variance parameters, which is particularly useful in the context of variational autoencoders. Lastly, it enables us to use stochastic gradient descent to optimize the parameters of our network, which is a key requirement for deep learning models.

The reparameterization trick is a powerful technique that has found widespread use in deep learning, especially in the context of generative models, where it plays a critical role in enabling efficient training and inference.

Example:

```
def reparameterize(self, mu, log_var):
    std = torch.exp(0.5*log_var) # standard deviation
    eps = torch.randn_like(std) # `eps` is a random tensor with elements drawn f
rom a standard normal distribution
    sample = mu + (eps * std) # shift and scale
    return sample
```

Code block 43

5.2.3 Decoder Network

The Decoder or Generative network plays an important role in the process of generating an output that matches the original input data. It takes the latent vector, which could either be the encoded input data or a sample from the latent space, and attempts to generate an output using a series of mathematical operations.

The decoder network's structure usually mirrors the encoder network, and is designed to be able to reconstruct the original input data as accurately as possible. This process involves using a combination of activation functions, weights, and biases to map the latent vector to the output space.

The decoder network may incorporate additional layers or features to improve the quality of the output, such as regularization techniques or dropout layers. By carefully designing the decoder network to work in tandem with the encoder network, it becomes possible to create a powerful generative model that can accurately generate new data points based on the original input data.

Example:

A simple decoder network for our VAE could look something like this:

```python
class Decoder(nn.Module):
    def __init__(self, z_dim, hidden_dim, output_dim):
        super().__init__()

        self.linear = nn.Linear(z_dim, hidden_dim)
        self.out = nn.Linear(hidden_dim, output_dim)

    def forward(self, x):
        hidden = F.relu(self.linear(x))
        predicted = torch.sigmoid(self.out(hidden))

        return predicted
```

Code block 44

The **Decoder** class defined here takes **z_dim** (latent space dimension), **hidden_dim** (hidden layer size), and **output_dim** (size of the output data). In the **forward** function, a linear transformation and a ReLU activation are applied to the input, and the output of the network is generated by applying a sigmoid function. This function ensures that the output values are in the range [0, 1], which is desired if we're working with images where pixel values are usually normalized to this range.

Example:

Now that we have the encoder and decoder, we can put them together to form the complete VAE model:

```python
class VAE(nn.Module):
    def __init__(self, input_dim, hidden_dim, z_dim):
        super().__init__()

        self.encoder = Encoder(input_dim, hidden_dim, z_dim)
        self.decoder = Decoder(z_dim, hidden_dim, input_dim)

    def forward(self, x):
        z_mu, z_var = self.encoder(x)
        z = self.reparameterize(z_mu, z_var)

        x_reconstructed = self.decoder(z)

        return x_reconstructed, z_mu, z_var

    def reparameterize(self, mu, log_var):
        std = torch.exp(0.5*log_var) # standard deviation
        eps = torch.randn_like(std) # `eps` is a random tensor with elements dra
wn from a standard normal distribution
        sample = mu + (eps * std) # shift and scale
        return sample
```

Code block 45

In this complete VAE model, the **forward** method first applies the encoder to the input **x** to get the mean and variance parameters of the latent space distribution. Then, it applies the reparameterization trick to sample a latent vector **z**, which is then fed into the decoder to generate the reconstructed output.

And there you have it - a simple Variational Autoencoder built in PyTorch! Of course, this is a very basic version of a VAE, and actual implementations might include more complex structures, multiple layers, convolutional layers if working with images, and additional techniques for regularization and optimization. But this should give you a good starting point to understanding the architectural aspects of VAEs.

In the next section, we'll delve into the training process of VAEs, where we'll see how the distinctive structure of VAEs informs the design of its unique loss function.

5.2.4 Variations in VAE Architectures

Variational Autoencoders (VAEs) are versatile and can be modified depending on the type of data or problem at hand. Here are a few variations:

Convolutional VAEs

When working with image data, VAEs can use convolutional layers, akin to Convolutional Neural Networks (CNNs). This modification allows the VAE to efficiently process and generate images by leveraging the inherent structure in image data. Thus, the encoder and decoder will be Convolutional Neural Networks.

Convolutional VAEs are particularly useful in image processing tasks as they are able to effectively handle the large amounts of information present in image data. By using convolutional layers, the VAE can break down the image into smaller, more manageable pieces, which can then be analyzed and reconstructed by the encoder and decoder. This approach not only allows for faster processing times, but also enables the VAE to generate higher quality images.

The use of convolutional layers in VAEs is a natural extension of the success of Convolutional Neural Networks in image classification tasks. By leveraging the same underlying structure of image data, Convolutional VAEs are able to achieve superior results compared to traditional VAEs when working with image data. Additionally, the encoder and decoder being Convolutional Neural Networks further improves the ability of the VAE to handle complex image data.

Convolutional VAEs are a valuable tool in image processing tasks, thanks to their ability to efficiently and effectively handle the large amounts of information present in image data. By leveraging the inherent structure of image data through the use of convolutional layers, Convolutional VAEs are able to generate high quality images and achieve superior results compared to traditional VAEs.

Recurrent VAEs

Recurrent Neural Networks (RNNs) are a type of neural network that have been successful in processing sequential data, such as time series or text. However, one major challenge with RNNs is that they struggle to learn long-term dependencies in the data.

This is where VAEs come in - by integrating the probabilistic framework of VAEs with the temporal modeling of RNNs, we can create Recurrent VAEs. Recurrent VAEs use recurrent layers, such as Long Short-Term Memory (LSTM) or Gated Recurrent Units (GRU), to model temporal dependencies in the data.

This not only makes VAEs more adept at handling sequential data, but also allows them to capture long-term dependencies in the data that RNNs struggle with. Overall, Recurrent VAEs provide a powerful tool for modeling complex, sequential data with both short-term and long-term dependencies.

Hybrid VAEs

In some cases, the architecture of VAEs can be a combination of both Convolutional and Recurrent layers. These hybrid models can be particularly effective for tasks such as video processing or 3D data, where there are both spatial and temporal correlations.

This is because Convolutional layers are good at capturing spatial correlations, while Recurrent layers are good at capturing temporal correlations. By combining the two, the hybrid VAE can learn to capture both types of correlations simultaneously.

These hybrid models can be used in a variety of applications, such as autonomous driving, where the model needs to process both image and lidar data. The hybrid VAE can learn to capture the spatial correlations in the image data, while also capturing the temporal correlations in the lidar data.

The hybrid VAE is a powerful tool for complex machine learning tasks that involve both spatial and temporal correlations.

Novel Architectural Innovations

As technology advances, researchers are constantly seeking new and innovative ways to improve the standard VAE architecture. These variations are usually designed to help better model specific types of data or to overcome certain challenges associated with training VAEs. For example, some researchers have experimented with adding additional layers to the VAE architecture to improve its performance on certain types of data.

Others have explored the use of attention mechanisms to help the VAE focus on important features in the data. Additionally, some researchers have developed novel loss functions that are better suited to certain types of data. All of these creative solutions demonstrate the ongoing commitment of researchers to advancing the field of VAEs and improving their ability to accurately model complex data.

While the basic architecture of a VAE—comprising an encoder, a latent space, and a decoder—remains constant, the specifics of how each of these components is implemented can greatly vary. Therefore, the aforementioned variations serve as good starting points, but as you delve deeper into the world of VAEs, you'll encounter a multitude of other architectures tailored to specific tasks and data types.

5.3 Training Variational Autoencoders (VAEs)

Training a Variational Autoencoder (VAE) follows a slightly different process compared to traditional neural networks. VAEs are an example of generative models that aim to learn the underlying distribution of the data.

Traditional neural networks, on the other hand, are discriminative models that aim to learn the decision boundary between different classes. VAEs have a unique architecture that consists of an encoder network, a decoder network, and a latent space. The encoder network maps the input data to the latent space, while the decoder network maps the latent space back to the input space.

The latent space is a key component of VAEs, as it enables the model to generate new data points that are similar to the training data. The specifics of the loss function of VAEs are also different from traditional neural networks. VAEs use a combination of a reconstruction loss and a KL divergence loss to ensure that the generated data points are both similar to the training data and that they are generated from the learned distribution.

The training process for VAEs involves the following steps:

5.3.1 Forward Pass

In order to generate the latent space distribution, the input data is passed through the encoder of the VAE, which consists of a series of layers that transform the data into a lower-dimensional representation. This representation is then used to compute the mean and log variance of the latent space distribution. The log variance is then converted into standard deviation so that the VAE can sample from the distribution and generate new data points.

It is important to note that the transformation of the data into a lower-dimensional representation is a crucial part of the VAE architecture. This is because the lower-dimensional representation captures the most important features of the data while discarding irrelevant details. This allows the VAE to generate new data points that are similar to the original data, but with some degree of variation.

The forward pass is just the first step in the VAE training process. Once the latent space distribution is generated, the next step is to sample from the distribution to generate new data points. This is done using the reparameterization trick, which allows the VAE to backpropagate through the sampling process and learn the optimal values for the encoder and decoder parameters.

5.3.2 Sampling from Latent Space

In order to generate new data, we must first obtain the parameters of the latent space distribution. This can be done using various methods, such as optimization or variational inference. Once we have these parameters, we can employ the reparameterization trick to sample from the distribution.

This involves sampling from a standard normal distribution, which is a commonly used distribution in statistics and machine learning. However, we must scale the sampled points by the standard deviation and shift them by the mean in order to obtain samples that are representative of the underlying distribution.

This scaling and shifting process is crucial in ensuring that the generated data is realistic and accurate. By using the reparameterization trick, we are able to efficiently sample from the latent space distribution and generate new data that is similar to the training data.

5.3.3 Decoding

In order to generate the reconstructed output, the points that were sampled from the latent space must first be passed through the decoder component of the VAE. This step is commonly referred to as "decoding". Essentially, the decoder takes the encoded points and transforms them back into a more interpretable format that retains the key information.

This process is essential for the success of the VAE, as it allows for the generation of high-quality outputs that are faithful to the original input. Without this crucial step, the VAE would be unable to generate meaningful results. Therefore, it is important to carefully consider the design of the decoder component in order to ensure that it is able to accurately and efficiently decode the sampled points.

5.3.4 Loss Calculation

Variational Autoencoders (VAEs) use a loss function that has two main components. The first component is the reconstruction loss, which evaluates how well the VAE can reconstruct the input data. This component is similar to that of other autoencoders. The second component is the KL divergence loss, which measures how closely the distribution of the latent space resembles a standard normal distribution. This is a crucial component of VAEs because it ensures that the latent space is well-behaved and can be easily sampled from. Without this component, the latent space could be chaotic and difficult to use for generating new data.

Additionally, it is worth noting that VAEs are a type of generative model that can be used to create new data. This is because the latent space is continuous and can be traversed to generate new samples. Furthermore, VAEs have been used successfully in many applications, including image and text generation, anomaly detection, and data compression. The ability to generate new data is particularly useful in applications where data is scarce or expensive to obtain, as it allows for the creation of synthetic data that can be used for training machine learning models.

Let's look at how this might look in code:

```python
class VAE(nn.Module):
    def __init__(self):
        super(VAE, self).__init__()

        # define the encoder and decoder networks
        self.encoder = ...
        self.decoder = ...

    def forward(self, x):
        mu, log_var = self.encoder(x)
        std = torch.exp(0.5*log_var)

        # reparameterization trick
        eps = torch.randn_like(std)
        z = mu + eps*std

        # decode
        recon_x = self.decoder(z)

        return recon_x, mu, log_var

def vae_loss(recon_x, x, mu, log_var):
    # reconstruction loss
    recon_loss = F.mse_loss(recon_x, x, reduction='sum')

    # KL divergence loss
    kld_loss = -0.5 * torch.sum(1 + log_var - mu.pow(2) - log_var.exp())

    return recon_loss + kld_loss

# instantiate VAE and optimizer
model = VAE()
optimizer = torch.optim.Adam(model.parameters(), lr=1e-3)

# training loop
for epoch in range(epochs):
    for batch in dataloader:
        # forward pass
        recon_batch, mu, log_var = model(batch)

        # loss
        loss = vae_loss(recon_batch, batch, mu, log_var)

        # backward pass
        optimizer.zero_grad()
        loss.backward()
        optimizer.step()
```

Code block 46

Please note that this code is a simplified version and a general representation of what VAE training might look like. The specifics might differ based on the architecture of the encoder and decoder, the loss function used, and other factors. Always tailor the code to the specifics of your task at hand.

5.3.5 Training Stability

Training Variational Autoencoders (VAEs) can sometimes be unstable, particularly in the early stages of training, which can lead to poor results. One of the reasons for this instability is that the Kullback-Leibler (KL) divergence term in the loss function can dominate, causing the network to ignore the reconstruction term.

A possible solution to this problem is to use a warm-up period where the weight of the KL divergence term in the loss function is gradually increased from 0 to 1. This can help stabilize training and improve results. However, it is important to note that the length of the warm-up period and the rate at which the weight is increased can vary depending on the specific VAE architecture and dataset being used. Additionally, other techniques such as annealing and free bits have also been proposed to address the issue of unstable training in VAEs.

5.3.6 Model Capacity

The capacity of the VAE, determined by the size and complexity of the encoder and decoder networks, can have a significant impact on the quality of the generated samples. If the model's capacity is too low, it might not be able to learn complex data distributions. This can lead to poor performance when generating new samples, as the model might not be able to capture the full range of variation in the data. On the other hand, if the capacity is too high, the model might overfit to the training data, which can lead to poor generalization performance on new data.

In order to find the right balance of model capacity, it is important to carefully tune the network architecture and hyperparameters. This can involve experimenting with different network sizes, activation functions, and regularization techniques. It may also involve adjusting the learning rate and other optimization parameters to ensure the model is learning effectively.

Another strategy for increasing model capacity is to use more advanced techniques, such as attention mechanisms or hierarchical structure. These techniques can allow the model to capture more complex relationships in the data, which can lead to better performance.

Finding the right model capacity is a critical aspect of getting good results with VAEs. It requires careful attention to the model architecture and hyperparameters, as well as a deep understanding of the underlying data distribution. By taking the time to carefully tune the model, researchers can ensure that their VAE is able to generate high-quality, diverse samples that capture the full range of variation in the data.

5.3.7 Choice of Prior

In the standard VAE, the prior is assumed to be a standard normal distribution. However, this is not always the best choice and it's possible to use other priors based on the specifics of the task. For instance, a mixture of Gaussians can be a better choice for certain tasks. Another possible approach is to use a hierarchical prior, which can better model the structure of the data.

The choice of prior can have a significant impact on the resulting model and its performance, so it's important to carefully consider the options and select the one that is most appropriate for the given task. Furthermore, the choice of prior can also affect the interpretability of the model and the insights that can be gained from analyzing it. Therefore, it's important to choose a prior that not only improves the performance of the model, but also aligns with the goals of the analysis.

Remember, the training process is an iterative one, and patience is crucial. It's unlikely that you'll get fantastic results on the first try, but with each iteration, your model should improve.

You can experiment with different configurations and settings to observe how they influence the model's performance. This iterative process of tweaking and testing is a core component of machine learning model development.

5.4 Evaluating VAEs

Evaluating the performance of Variational Autoencoders (VAEs) is a complex task that requires several metrics and methods. In order to accurately interpret the performance of your VAE and improve its results, it is important to have a thorough understanding of these evaluation techniques. One commonly used metric is the reconstruction error, which measures the difference between the original data and the data generated by the VAE.

Another important metric is the KL divergence, which measures the distance between the distribution of the encoded data and the prior distribution. The performance of a VAE can be evaluated by analyzing the quality of the generated samples, the diversity of the generated data, and the ability of the VAE to interpolate between data points.

By carefully considering these metrics and methods, you can gain a deeper understanding of the performance of your VAE and make informed decisions about how to improve its results.

5.4.1 Reconstruction Loss

The primary metric used to evaluate a VAE's performance is the reconstruction loss. This metric is crucial in determining the effectiveness of the model's ability to reconstruct the input data. The reconstruction loss is calculated by comparing the original input and the reconstructed output.

The lower the reconstruction loss, the more accurate the VAE can reproduce the input data. In addition, there are two common methods for calculating the reconstruction loss: mean squared error for continuous data and cross-entropy for binary data.

These two methods are used to evaluate the model's accuracy in reconstructing the input data, which is an essential aspect of VAEs. Therefore, it is important to ensure that the reconstruction loss is minimized to achieve the best possible results.

Example:

Here's a basic example of how to compute the reconstruction loss in Python using Mean Squared Error:

```python
from keras.losses import mean_squared_error

def compute_reconstruction_loss(original, reconstructed):
    # Ensure the data is in float format for accurate loss calculation
    original = original.astype('float32')
    reconstructed = reconstructed.astype('float32')

    # Compute the mean squared error between the original data and the reconstru
cted data
    mse = mean_squared_error(original, reconstructed)

    # Return the mean of the MSE values
    return tf.reduce_mean(mse)
```

Code block 47

5.4.2 KL Divergence

VAEs, or Variational Autoencoders, are a commonly used type of neural network in deep learning. They are used to learn a low-dimensional representation of high-dimensional data by encoding the input data into a lower-dimensional vector space.

While the reconstruction error is one commonly used metric to evaluate VAEs, it is not the only one. Another important metric is the Kullback-Leibler (KL) Divergence. This measures how closely the learned latent variable distribution aligns with the prior distribution (typically a standard normal distribution).

The KL divergence is used in the loss function of VAEs to ensure that the distribution of the latent variables matches the prior distribution. Lower KL divergence means that the distributions are more similar. Therefore, it is important to optimize this metric in order to achieve a better performance of VAEs.

In addition, there are also other metrics that can be used to evaluate VAEs, such as the generation quality of the generated samples and the ability to learn meaningful representations in the latent space.

Example:

```
def compute_kl_divergence(mean, logvar):
    kl_loss = -0.5 * tf.reduce_sum(1 + logvar - tf.square(mean) - tf.exp(logva
r), axis=-1)
    return tf.reduce_mean(kl_loss)
```

Code block 48

In this function, we compute the KL divergence for each sample in the batch and then take the mean. The **logvar** variable represents the log variance of the latent variable distribution. This is used instead of the standard deviation or variance for numerical stability reasons.

5.4.3 Sample Quality and Diversity

One additional evaluation method for VAEs is to generate new samples and assess their quality. While quality is subjective and depends on the task at hand, for image generation, one might evaluate the visual appeal and realism of the generated images.

However, quality is not the only factor to consider when evaluating the effectiveness of a VAE. It is also important to assess the diversity of the generated samples. A successful VAE should be able to generate samples that represent different modes of the data distribution, ensuring a wide variety of samples. This is especially important for tasks where there is a lot of variation in the data, as the model needs to be able to capture all the different features and nuances.

Moreover, while generating new samples is a useful evaluation method, it is important to also consider other metrics such as reconstruction error, latent space interpolation, and disentanglement of the learned representations. By considering a variety of evaluation metrics, we can gain a more holistic understanding of the performance of the VAE and make informed decisions about how to improve it.

5.4.4 Latent Space Interpolation

VAEs are a fascinating area of research in the field of machine learning. One of their unique properties is their ability to construct a latent space that is both smooth and meaningful. This is particularly useful when generating new samples based on data that the VAE has learned.

One way to evaluate the quality of the VAE's latent space is by interpolating between different points in the space. By doing this, we can ensure that the transitions between the generated samples are smooth and make sense.

Moreover, this smoothness in the latent space can be used to generate new and diverse samples that are not present in the original data set. This is a powerful tool for many applications, such as image and speech generation, where having a diverse set of samples is crucial. VAEs are a promising area of research that has the potential to revolutionize the field of machine learning and beyond.

Example:

Here is a simple code example for performing latent space interpolation between two randomly chosen points:

```python
def interpolate_latent_space(vae, point1, point2, num_steps):
    # Compute the latent representations for point1 and point2
    z_point1 = vae.encode(point1)[0]
    z_point2 = vae.encode(point2)[0]

    # Compute the interpolation steps
    interpolation_steps = np.linspace(0, 1, num_steps)

    # Interpolate between the latent representations and decode the interpolated
representations
    interpolated_images = []
    for step in interpolation_steps:
        z_interpolated = z_point1 * (1 - step) + z_point2 * step
        interpolated_image = vae.decode(z_interpolated[np.newaxis, :])
        interpolated_images.append(interpolated_image)

    return interpolated_images
```

Code block 49

In this code, **vae.encode(point)[0]** returns the mean of the latent representation for the given point. Then, we linearly interpolate between the latent representations of **point1** and **point2** for a given number of steps. For each interpolated point in the latent space, we generate a new image by decoding the interpolated latent representation. The output is a list of interpolated images.

You would visualize the results of this interpolation as follows:

```python
point1, point2 = np.random.choice(len(test_dataset), 2)
num_steps = 10

interpolated_images = interpolate_latent_space(vae, test_dataset[point1], test_d
ataset[point2], num_steps)

plt.figure(figsize=(10, 2))
for i, img in enumerate(interpolated_images):
    plt.subplot(1, num_steps, i + 1)
    plt.imshow(img.squeeze(), cmap='gray')
    plt.axis('off')
plt.show()
```

Code block 50

The above code selects two random points from the test dataset, performs interpolation, and visualizes the resulting images. Please note that the visualization assumes grayscale images (i.e., single channel). If you are working with color images, you might need to adjust the visualization code accordingly.

This exercise provides an excellent way to understand the landscape of the latent space that the VAE learns and to see how it captures the meaningful variations in your dataset.

5.4.5 Fréchet Inception Distance (FID) Score

In addition to the qualitative and quantitative measures discussed, another quantitative measure commonly used in practice is the Fréchet Inception Distance (FID) Score. This score calculates the distance between the statistics of the generated samples and those of the real samples.

These scores have limitations and do not always perfectly correlate with perceived image quality. Hence, subjective human evaluation is often employed in practice, which, though time-consuming and expensive, provides valuable feedback on the visual quality of the generated samples.

To calculate the FID score, you can make use of the Inception model from TensorFlow's Keras API. Here is a python code example of how you can calculate FID score assuming you're working with image data:

```python
import tensorflow as tf
from scipy.linalg import sqrtm
from keras.applications.inception_v3 import InceptionV3
from keras.applications.inception_v3 import preprocess_input

# calculate frechet inception distance
def calculate_fid(model, images1, images2):
    # calculate activations
    act1 = model.predict(images1)
    act2 = model.predict(images2)
    # calculate mean and covariance statistics
    mu1, sigma1 = act1.mean(axis=0), np.cov(act1, rowvar=False)
    mu2, sigma2 = act2.mean(axis=0), np.cov(act2, rowvar=False)
    # calculate sum squared difference between means
    ssdiff = np.sum((mu1 - mu2)**2.0)
    # calculate sqrt of product between cov
    covmean = sqrtm(sigma1.dot(sigma2))
    # check and correct imaginary numbers from sqrt
    if np.iscomplexobj(covmean):
        covmean = covmean.real
    # calculate score
    fid = ssdiff + np.trace(sigma1 + sigma2 - 2.0 * covmean)
    return fid

# prepare the inception v3 model
model = InceptionV3(include_top=False, pooling='avg', input_shape=(299,299,3))
# define two collections of images
images1 = ... # real images
images2 = ... # generated images
# pre-process images
images1 = preprocess_input(images1)
images2 = preprocess_input(images2)
# fid between images1 and images2
fid = calculate_fid(model, images1, images2)
print('FID: %.3f' % fid)
```

Code block 51

This code will give you a numerical value (FID score) which gives an indication of the similarity between the distribution of generated images and real images, with lower values indicating greater similarity. However, these quantitative measures should be used in combination with other evaluation methods and not be the sole deciding factor of a model's quality. They should serve as a guideline rather than the final verdict on the performance of the VAE model.

Remember to be mindful of the inherent randomness in training generative models and to perform multiple runs or use different seeds to get a better understanding of your model's performance.

5.5 Variations of VAEs

Variational Autoencoders (VAEs) have become increasingly popular in recent years due to their ability to generate new data while preserving the underlying structure of the original data distribution. As a result, researchers have introduced a range of variations tailored to specific tasks. For example, some researchers have introduced modifications to address issues related to image generation, while others have focused on improving the model's performance for natural language processing tasks.

One significant variant of VAEs is the Conditional Variational Autoencoder (CVAE), which takes into account the input data's conditional dependencies. Another variant is the Adversarial Autoencoder (AAE), which introduces an adversarial training objective to improve the generated samples' quality. There are VAE variants that incorporate recurrent neural networks (RNNs) to model sequences, such as the Variational Recurrent Autoencoder (VRAE) and the Hierarchical Variational Recurrent Autoencoder (HVRNN).

The adaptability of VAEs has led to a wide range of variations that can be tailored to specific domains and tasks. As the field of deep learning continues to evolve, it is likely that we will see even more variations on this powerful architecture emerge.

5.5.1 Conditional Variational Autoencoder (CVAE)

A Conditional Variational Autoencoder (CVAE) is a type of VAE that conditions the generation process on certain attributes to generate data based on a particular class or feature. In contrast with the standard VAE, which generates random data, the CVAE generates data that corresponds to a specific class. This is especially useful in image datasets, where a CVAE can generate images of a specific type of fruit given that fruit's label as a condition.

For example, the CVAE can generate images of apples, oranges, and bananas, using their respective labels as conditions. This is achieved by encoding the input image and the conditioning label into a latent representation, which is then decoded into a new image. This process ensures that the generated images are more precise and accurate than those generated by a standard VAE.

Moreover, CVAEs can be used in various applications such as generative modeling, image classification, and natural language processing. CVAEs have shown promising results in image-to-image translation, where an input image is translated to an output image based on a specific condition. For example, a CVAE can be trained to translate a black and white image to a colored image, given the color as a condition.

CVAEs are a powerful extension of VAEs that allow for more precise and accurate data generation by conditioning on certain attributes. They have numerous applications in various fields and have demonstrated impressive results in image-to-image translation.

Example:

Here's a basic outline of how you might implement a CVAE in Python:

```python
class CVAE(tf.keras.Model):
    """Conditional Variational Autoencoder"""

    def __init__(self, latent_dim):
        super(CVAE, self).__init__()
        self.latent_dim = latent_dim
        self.encoder = tf.keras.Sequential([
          # ... (define encoder layers)
        ])
        self.decoder = tf.keras.Sequential([
          # ... (define decoder layers)
        ])

    def call(self, x, conditioning):
        encoded = self.encoder(tf.concat([x, conditioning], axis=-1))
        decoded = self.decoder(encoded)
        return decoded
```

Code block 52

5.5.2 Adversarial Autoencoders (AAEs)

Adversarial Autoencoders (AAEs) are a type of neural network that combines the ideas of Variational Autoencoders (VAEs) and Generative Adversarial Networks (GANs). AAEs use an adversarial training strategy to shape the distribution of the latent vector, forcing it to match a prior distribution, which is typically a Gaussian distribution.

This adversarial training process involves two neural networks - a generator and a discriminator - which are trained simultaneously. The generator is responsible for generating a latent vector that can be decoded by the decoder network to produce an output that resembles the input data. On the other hand, the discriminator network tries to distinguish between the generated latent vectors and the real latent vectors.

By using this adversarial training process, AAEs can achieve better disentanglement of the factors of variation in the latent vector. This improved disentanglement can be helpful in many tasks, like data generation, anomaly detection, and more. Moreover, it can also lead to the creation of more realistic images, which can be useful in applications such as computer vision and image processing.

5.5.3 β-VAEs

A β-VAE, or beta-VAE, is a variation of the VAE, or variational autoencoder, that introduces a coefficient to the KL divergence term in the loss function. This coefficient, which is usually referred to as β, can be modified to achieve a balance between the two components of the loss, namely the reconstruction loss and the KL divergence.

By adjusting the value of β, one can influence the degree of disentanglement in the learned representations. Specifically, a higher β encourages more disentanglement among the factors of variation, which can be beneficial in certain scenarios, such as when the input data is complex or high-dimensional. However, increasing β can also come at a cost, as it may lead to a higher reconstruction error, which can impact the overall performance of the model.

In practice, selecting the appropriate value of β for a given task or dataset requires careful experimentation and evaluation. Researchers have proposed various methods for automatically tuning β based on heuristics or optimization techniques, but these approaches are not universally applicable and may require additional resources or expertise.

5.5.4 Implementing a Conditional Variational Autoencoder (CVAE)

As an application of what we have learned so far, let's delve deeper into the topic of CVAEs. Conditional Variational Autoencoders (CVAEs) are a powerful technique that allows us to generate data based on specific criteria. CVAEs are particularly useful for image generation tasks, such as generating images of digits. One of the key benefits of CVAEs is that they allow us to generate images of any digit we specify. This is particularly useful in applications where we want to generate images of specific numbers. For instance, we might want to generate images of the number "9" to train a computer vision algorithm to detect the digit "9" in images.

To implement a CVAE, we need to first understand the underlying principles. CVAEs are a type of neural network that combine elements of both autoencoders and variational autoencoders. They are trained on data that has specific conditions or labels attached to it. These conditions are typically encoded as a vector, which is fed into the network along with the input data. The network then learns to generate data that meets those conditions.

For the purpose of this exercise, we will create a CVAE that can generate MNIST images of a digit that we specify. MNIST is a well-known dataset of handwritten digits, used extensively in the field of computer vision. By generating MNIST images of a specific digit, we can test the capabilities of our CVAE and see how well it performs. We will start by training the CVAE on the MNIST dataset, and then move on to generating images of specific digits. The process of creating a CVAE involves several steps, including defining the architecture of the network, choosing appropriate loss functions, and tuning hyperparameters. By following these steps, we can create a CVAE that is capable of generating high-quality images of specific digits.

Firstly, let's create the encoder and decoder networks, both of which will be simple feed-forward neural networks:

```python
class CVAE(tf.keras.Model):
    def __init__(self, latent_dim):
        super(CVAE, self).__init__()
        self.latent_dim = latent_dim
        self.encoder = tf.keras.Sequential(
            [
                tf.keras.layers.InputLayer(input_shape=(28, 28, 1)),
                tf.keras.layers.Conv2D(filters=32, kernel_size=3, strides=(2,
2), activation='relu'),
                tf.keras.layers.Conv2D(filters=64, kernel_size=3, strides=(2,
2), activation='relu'),
                tf.keras.layers.Flatten(),
                # No activation
                tf.keras.layers.Dense(latent_dim + latent_dim),
            ]
        )

        self.decoder = tf.keras.Sequential(
            [
                tf.keras.layers.InputLayer(input_shape=(latent_dim,)),
                tf.keras.layers.Dense(units=7*7*32, activation=tf.nn.relu),
                tf.keras.layers.Reshape(target_shape=(7, 7, 32)),
                tf.keras.layers.Conv2DTranspose(filters=64, kernel_size=3, strid
es=2, padding='same',
                                                activation='relu'),
                tf.keras.layers.Conv2DTranspose(filters=32, kernel_size=3, strid
es=2, padding='same',
                                                activation='relu'),
                # No activation
                tf.keras.layers.Conv2DTranspose(filters=1, kernel_size=3, stride
s=1, padding='same'),
            ]
        )
```

Code block 53

This is a basic setup where the encoder takes as input a 28x28 image, and the decoder produces a 28x28 image. Note that we use convolutional layers for the encoder and transposed convolutions for the decoder, which is a common architecture for VAEs working with images.

Now, let's define the **reparameterize** method, which is crucial for the VAE:

```
def reparameterize(self, mean, logvar):
    eps = tf.random.normal(shape=mean.shape)
    return eps * tf.exp(logvar * .5) + mean
```

Code block 54

This method generates a random latent vector in the region specified by the mean and variance.

Finally, we implement the **call** method that defines the forward pass of our model:

```
def call(self, x):
    mean, logvar = tf.split(self.encoder(x), num_or_size_splits=2, axis=1)
    z = self.reparameterize(mean, logvar)
    x_recon = self.decoder(z)
    return x_recon
```

Code block 55

In the above code, the encoder network outputs the parameters of the Gaussian distribution. The **reparameterize** method is then used to sample from this distribution, and the sampled vector **z** is passed to the decoder to generate the output.

Now, you have a complete CVAE model that you can train on the MNIST dataset. To generate a new sample given a condition (a digit), you would simply feed this condition along with the input to the encoder and decoder.

5.6 Use Cases and Applications of Variational Autoencoders (VAEs)

VAEs have diverse applications across various domains. Below are some of the notable uses of VAEs:

5.6.1 Anomaly Detection

Anomaly detection refers to the task of identifying unusual data points in a dataset. Given their ability to reconstruct inputs and measure the reconstruction loss, VAEs are a perfect fit for this task. The idea is to train a VAE on normal data and use it to reconstruct new data. If the new data is normal, it should be reconstructed well (with small reconstruction error). However, if the new data is an anomaly, it should be reconstructed poorly (with large reconstruction error).

```python
# Assume vae_model is a trained Variational Autoencoder

def anomaly_score(data, vae_model):
    reconstructed_data, _, _ = vae_model(data)
    reconstruction_error = torch.nn.functional.mse_loss(data, reconstructed_dat
a)
    return reconstruction_error.item()

# Now you can use this anomaly_score function to score new data
```

Code block 56

5.6.2 Image Generation

VAEs are also used to generate new images that resemble the training set. This is done by sampling from the latent space and then decoding the sampled vector to an image.

```python
# Assume vae_model is a trained Variational Autoencoder

def generate_image(vae_model):
    z = torch.randn(1, vae_model.latent_dim)
    generated_image = vae_model.decode(z)
    return generated_image

# Now you can use this generate_image function to create new images
```

Code block 57

5.6.3 Drug Discovery

In the field of medicine, VAEs or Variational Autoencoders have become an increasingly popular tool for drug discovery. VAEs work by encoding the chemical structure of known drug molecules into a lower-dimensional space, or latent space, where they can be more easily manipulated. This encoding process allows the VAE to learn patterns in the data which can then be used to generate new molecules with similar structures.

Once the molecules are encoded, the VAE is able to decode random points from the latent space to generate new potential drug molecules. These new molecules are then analyzed to determine if they have the desired properties for use as medications. This process can be repeated multiple times with the VAE generating and refining new molecules until satisfactory results are obtained.

=VAEs offer a promising approach to drug discovery by providing a way to generate new molecules for testing in a more efficient and targeted manner.

5.6.4 Music Generation

In the domain of music, Variational Autoencoders (VAEs) can be trained on a wide range of musical data, including musical notes, audio recordings, and even MIDI files. VAEs are a type of neural network that is specifically designed to compress and decompress data, making them an ideal tool for generating new music.

During training, VAEs learn the underlying structure of the music that they are working with. This means that they can identify patterns and relationships between different musical elements, such as notes and chords. Once the model has been trained, it can be used to generate new music that resembles the training set.

One of the most exciting aspects of using VAEs for music generation is the ability to explore new musical ideas and styles. By tweaking the parameters of the model or feeding it different input data, musicians and composers can create new and unique pieces of music that would have been difficult to create otherwise.

VAEs are a powerful tool for music generation that offer a high degree of flexibility and creativity. As the field of machine learning continues to evolve, we can expect to see even more impressive applications of VAEs in the world of music and beyond.

These applications show the breadth of VAEs' capabilities. With their unique architecture and the use of a probabilistic approach, they offer exciting possibilities for researchers and practitioners alike.

5.7 Practical Exercises

1. **Building a VAE:** Implement a simple Variational Autoencoder in PyTorch. The architecture can be quite simple: for instance, you could use a couple of fully connected layers for the encoder and the decoder.

```python
class VAE(nn.Module):
    def __init__(self):
        super(VAE, self).__init__()

        # Define the architecture for your VAE here

    def encode(self, x):
        # Implement the encoding part here

    def reparameterize(self, mu, logvar):
        # Implement the reparameterization trick here

    def decode(self, z):
        # Implement the decoding part here

    def forward(self, x):
        # Define the forward pass for your VAE here
```

Code block 58

2. **Training a VAE:** After implementing the VAE, the next step is to train it on a dataset. You could use a simple dataset like MNIST for this purpose. Pay attention to how you define your loss function, remember that it's a combination of a reconstruction loss and a KL-divergence loss.

3. **Exploring the Latent Space:** After training your VAE, use it to explore the latent space. Generate some random vectors, pass them through the decoder, and observe the outputs. Do they resemble the training data?

4. **Interpolation in the Latent Space:** Another interesting exercise is to perform interpolation in the latent space. Start from the latent vector of one example, and gradually transform it into the latent vector of another example. Decode the intermediate vectors and observe the outputs. Do you see a smooth transition from one example to another?

5. **Anomaly Detection:** Use your trained VAE for anomaly detection. Train your VAE on one class of the MNIST dataset and test it on another class. Can your VAE detect the anomalies?

These exercises should provide a good practice to understand the workings of VAEs in depth. You can also try implementing different variations of VAEs and observe the changes in performance and outputs.

Chapter 5 Conclusion

In this chapter, we have embarked on an in-depth journey into the world of Variational Autoencoders (VAEs), one of the most fascinating branches in the field of generative models.

We started by understanding the fundamental concept behind VAEs: to build a probabilistic, generative model that represents data in a latent distribution. We saw that the real strength of VAEs lies in their ability to learn complex, high-dimensional distributions, and then generate new data that looks as if it has been drawn from the same distribution as the training data.

We dissected the architecture of VAEs, discussing the significance of the encoder, the decoder, and the reparameterization trick that allows the model to backpropagate through random nodes. We then dove into the training process, which involves a delicate balance between reconstruction loss and KL divergence, aiming to produce a model that not only generates high-quality data but also ensures that the latent variables are well-distributed.

Further, we studied various variations of VAEs, such as Conditional VAEs, β-VAEs, and VAE-GAN hybrids, that introduce exciting twists to the standard model and provide more control and flexibility over the generative process.

The discussion on use-cases and applications showed the versatility of VAEs. From generating new faces, enhancing creativity in the field of art, to anomaly detection in healthcare and financial sectors, the possibilities with VAEs are boundless.

Lastly, we provided practical exercises to help you implement and experiment with VAEs. The knowledge and the hands-on experience from these exercises are invaluable, as they lay the foundation for advanced topics and projects involving VAEs, such as the next chapter - Handwritten Digit Generation with VAEs.

As we close this chapter, it is important to remember that the field of VAEs is rich and continually evolving. The concepts, techniques, and models discussed here are by no means exhaustive, and you are encouraged to delve deeper into this exciting domain.

In the next chapter, we will apply the knowledge acquired here to a real-world project. Let's move on to generating handwritten digits with VAEs!

Chapter 6: Project: Handwritten Digit Generation with VAEs

Welcome to Chapter 6! In this chapter, we will put theory into practice by working on a project to generate handwritten digits using Variational Autoencoders (VAEs). This project will serve as a hands-on guide and reinforcement of the concepts we have learned in the previous chapter.

Creating a model capable of generating realistic handwritten digits could find applications in a number of areas, from data augmentation for improving performance of other machine learning models, to solving CAPTCHA challenges, to simply demonstrating the power of generative models in a visually impressive way.

The chapter will proceed as follows:

1. Data Collection and Preprocessing
2. Model Creation
3. Training the VAE
4. Generating New Digits
5. Evaluation and Conclusion

Let's get started!

6.1 Data Collection and Preprocessing

6.1.1 Dataset Selection

For the purpose of this project, we will use the MNIST (Modified National Institute of Standards and Technology) dataset. This is a widely used dataset for machine learning projects and consists of 70,000 28x28 grayscale images of the ten digits, along with their corresponding labels.

The MNIST dataset is easily accessible through several deep-learning libraries such as TensorFlow and PyTorch.

Here's how to load it using TensorFlow:

```python
from tensorflow.keras.datasets import mnist

# the data, split between train and test sets
(x_train, y_train), (x_test, y_test) = mnist.load_data()
```

Code block 59

6.1.2 Data Preprocessing

The images in the MNIST dataset are grayscale, with pixel values ranging from 0 to 255. Before feeding them into our VAE, we need to normalize these values to a range between 0 and 1. This can easily be achieved by dividing the images by 255.

Additionally, as we will be working with a VAE, we do not need the labels that come with the dataset, so we can safely ignore them.

```python
# Reshape and normalize
x_train = x_train.astype('float32') / 255.
x_test = x_test.astype('float32') / 255.
```

Code block 60

Since the VAE architecture we'll implement takes inputs in a flat, vectorized format, we also need to reshape each image from its original 2D form (28x28 pixels) to a 1D form (784 pixels).

```python
x_train = x_train.reshape((len(x_train), np.prod(x_train.shape[1:])))
x_test = x_test.reshape((len(x_test), np.prod(x_test.shape[1:])))
```

Code block 61

After this preprocessing, our data is ready to be fed into a VAE. In the next sections, we will look into how to design the VAE architecture, train the model, and finally, generate new handwritten digits.

6.2 Model Creation

The next step in our project is the creation of the Variational Autoencoder model. As we learned in Chapter 5, the VAE consists of an encoder, a decoder, and a loss function that incorporates a reconstruction term as well as a Kullback-Leibler divergence term.

Let's create these components using TensorFlow and Keras.

6.2.1 Encoder

The encoder part of the VAE is responsible for mapping the input data into a latent space representation. This is typically done using a neural network.

Here's an example of how we might define the encoder using Keras:

```python
import tensorflow as tf
from tensorflow.keras import layers

original_dim = 28 * 28
intermediate_dim = 64
latent_dim = 2

# Define encoder model
inputs = tf.keras.Input(shape=(original_dim,))
h = layers.Dense(intermediate_dim, activation='relu')(inputs)
z_mean = layers.Dense(latent_dim)(h)
z_log_sigma = layers.Dense(latent_dim)(h)
```

Code block 62

In the code above, we first define the dimensions of our data and the latent space. Then, we define the structure of the encoder network. Our encoder model has a single hidden layer with a ReLU activation function. The encoder outputs the parameters of a Gaussian distribution, **z_mean** and **z_log_sigma**.

6.2.2 Latent Space Sampling

We will sample from the latent space to generate a new data point. We do this by adding a custom layer that takes **z_mean** and **z_log_sigma** as input and outputs a random sample from the corresponding Gaussian distribution.

```python
from tensorflow.keras import backend as K

def sampling(args):
    z_mean, z_log_sigma = args
    epsilon = K.random_normal(shape=(K.shape(z_mean)[0], latent_dim),
                              mean=0., stddev=1.)
    return z_mean + K.exp(z_log_sigma) * epsilon

z = layers.Lambda(sampling)([z_mean, z_log_sigma])
```

Code block 63

6.2.3 Decoder

The decoder part of the VAE takes a point in the latent space and maps it back to the original data space. Like the encoder, the decoder is also typically implemented as a neural network.

Here's how we might define the decoder:

```python
# Define decoder model
decoder_h = layers.Dense(intermediate_dim, activation='relu')
decoder_mean = layers.Dense(original_dim, activation='sigmoid')
h_decoded = decoder_h(z)
x_decoded_mean = decoder_mean(h_decoded)
```

Code block 64

In this code, we define the structure of the decoder network. Our decoder model also has a single hidden layer with a ReLU activation function. The output layer uses a sigmoid activation function to ensure that the output values fall within the range [0, 1], the same range as our normalized input data.

6.2.4 Assembling the VAE

We now have all the components needed for our VAE: an encoder that maps our data to a latent space, a decoder that maps from the latent space back to the data space, and a sampling function that allows us to generate new data points in the latent space.

We can now assemble these components into a single model:

```python
from tensorflow.keras import Model

# Assemble encoder, sampler and decoder into a VAE model
vae = Model(inputs, x_decoded_mean)

# Print model summary
vae.summary()
```

Code block 65

Our VAE model is now ready to be compiled and trained, which we will cover in the next section.

6.3 Training the VAE

After we have assembled our Variational Autoencoder (VAE), the next step is to compile and train the model on our data.

6.3.1 Compiling the VAE

Before we can train our VAE, we need to compile it. As part of the compilation process, we need to specify a loss function and an optimizer.

The loss function for VAEs is a bit different from the loss functions we've seen so far. It consists of two parts:

1. A reconstruction loss that encourages the decoder to recreate the input data as accurately as possible, and
2. A KL divergence loss that pushes the distribution of the latent space to approximate a standard normal distribution.

Let's define this loss function:

```python
from tensorflow.keras import backend as K

def vae_loss(x, x_decoded_mean):
    xent_loss = original_dim * tf.keras.losses.binary_crossentropy(x, x_decoded_mean)
    kl_loss = - 0.5 * K.sum(1 + z_log_sigma - K.square(z_mean) - K.exp(z_log_sigma), axis=-1)
    return K.mean(xent_loss + kl_loss)
```

Code block 66

In this code, **xent_loss** is the reconstruction loss and **kl_loss** is the KL divergence loss. We calculate the mean of these losses across the batch to get the final loss value.

Next, we compile the model:

```python
# Compile VAE model
vae.compile(optimizer='rmsprop', loss=vae_loss)
```

Code block 67

6.3.2 Training the VAE

Once our model is compiled, we can train it on our data. Here's how we might do this:

```python
# Train the VAE
vae.fit(x_train, x_train,
        shuffle=True,
        epochs=50,
        batch_size=batch_size,
        validation_data=(x_test, x_test))
```

Code block 68

In this code, we're calling the **fit** method of our VAE model and passing in our training data **x_train** as both the input and the target data. This is because we want our VAE to learn to recreate its input data.

We're also passing a few additional arguments:

- **shuffle=True**: This shuffles our data before each epoch, which can help to avoid patterns and dependencies that might arise from the order of the data points.
- **epochs=50**: This tells Keras to run the training process for 50 epochs.
- **batch_size=batch_size**: This specifies the number of samples per gradient update.
- **validation_data=(x_test, x_test)**: This is our validation data, which Keras will use to evaluate the loss and any model metrics at the end of each epoch. This allows us to see how well our model is doing without touching the test data.

After running this code, our VAE should be trained and ready to generate new handwritten digits!

Remember that this is just a simple example. In practice, we might want to use more sophisticated techniques such as early stopping, learning rate decay, or other forms of regularization to improve the training process and the final model.

6.4 Generating New Handwritten Digits

Now that our Variational Autoencoder (VAE) is trained, we can use it to generate new, artificial handwritten digits. The process of generating new data with a VAE involves two main steps:

1. Sampling points from the latent space.
2. Decoding these points back into the original data space.

6.4.1 Sampling Points from the Latent Space

The first step in the generation process is to sample points from the latent space. As we recall, the latent space of a VAE is a compressed, abstract representation of our data, and it's where the VAE learns to encode the most important features and structures of our data.

In our case, we've structured our VAE so that the latent space follows a standard normal distribution. This means we can generate new points simply by sampling from this distribution.

Here's a Python function that samples a given number of points from the latent space:

```python
import numpy as np

def sample_latent_points(latent_dim, n_samples):
    # Generate points in the latent space
    x_input = np.random.randn(latent_dim * n_samples)

    # Reshape into a batch of inputs for the network
    x_input = x_input.reshape(n_samples, latent_dim)

    return x_input
```

Code block 69

This function takes the dimensionality of the latent space and the number of samples we want to generate as arguments, and returns a batch of points sampled from the standard normal distribution.

6.4.2 Decoding Points from the Latent Space

The second step in the generation process is to decode the points we've sampled from the latent space back into the original data space. This is done by passing the points through the decoder part of our VAE.

Here's a Python function that uses our VAE's decoder to generate new handwritten digits from points in the latent space:

```python
def generate_digits(decoder, latent_dim, n_samples):
    # Sample points in the latent space
    x_input = sample_latent_points(latent_dim, n_samples)

    # Predict outputs given the points in the latent space
    images = decoder.predict(x_input)

    return images
```

Code block 70

In this function, we first sample a batch of points from the latent space using the **sample_latent_points** function we defined earlier. We then pass these points through the decoder part of our VAE to generate new handwritten digits.

With these functions, we can generate any number of new, artificial handwritten digits that resemble the real digits our VAE was trained on. Note that since the generation process involves random sampling from the latent space, the generated digits will be different each time we run the function.

6.5 Evaluating the Model

Evaluating generative models like Variational Autoencoders (VAEs) is not as straightforward as evaluating other types of models such as classifiers. With classifiers, we can use metrics like accuracy, precision, and recall because we have a clear target to compare our model's predictions with. But with generative models, we usually don't have a clear target to compare our generated data to.

However, we can still evaluate our model qualitatively and quantitatively.

6.5.1 Qualitative Evaluation

The easiest way to evaluate our model is by visually inspecting the images it generates. We can generate a few samples and see if they look like plausible handwritten digits.

```python
import matplotlib.pyplot as plt

# Generate 25 random digits
digits = generate_digits(decoder, latent_dim, 25)

# Plot the generated digits
fig, axes = plt.subplots(5, 5, figsize=(10,10))

for i, ax in enumerate(axes.flat):
    ax.imshow(digits[i].reshape(28, 28), cmap='gray')
    ax.axis('off')

plt.show()
```

Code block 71

The above code generates 25 random handwritten digits using our model and then plots them using **matplotlib**. This gives us a quick and easy way to inspect our generated digits and see if they look realistic.

6.5.2 Quantitative Evaluation

For a more objective evaluation, we can use metrics such as the Frechet Inception Distance (FID). The FID measures the distance between the distribution of the generated images and the distribution of the real images. A lower FID indicates that the two distributions are closer, which means our generated images are more similar to the real images.

Here's a simple implementation of FID:

```python
from scipy.linalg import sqrtm
from keras.applications.inception_v3 import InceptionV3
from keras.applications.inception_v3 import preprocess_input
from keras.datasets import mnist
from skimage.transform import resize
from numpy import cov
from numpy import trace
from numpy import iscomplexobj
from numpy import asarray
from numpy.random import randint

# scale an array of images to a new size
def scale_images(images, new_shape):
    images_list = list()
    for image in images:
        # resize with nearest neighbor interpolation
        new_image = resize(image, new_shape, 0)
        # store
        images_list.append(new_image)
    return asarray(images_list)

# calculate frechet inception distance
def calculate_fid(model, images1, images2):
    # calculate activations
    act1 = model.predict(images1)
    act2 = model.predict(images2)
    # calculate mean and covariance statistics
    mu1, sigma1 = act1.mean(axis=0), cov(act1, rowvar=False)
    mu2, sigma2 = act2.mean(axis=0), cov(act2, rowvar=False)
    # calculate sum squared difference between means
    ssdiff = np.sum((mu1 - mu2)**2.0)
    # calculate sqrt of product between cov
    covmean = sqrtm(sigma1.dot(sigma2))
    # check and correct imaginary numbers from sqrt
    if iscomplexobj(covmean):
        covmean = covmean.real
    # calculate score
    fid = ssdiff + trace(sigma1 + sigma2 - 2.0 * covmean)
    return fid
```

Code block 72

In the above code, **calculate_fid** is the main function that calculates the FID between two sets of images. It first calculates the activations of the images using the InceptionV3 model. Then, it calculates the mean and covariance of the activations

6.6 Example of Full Code for the Project

In the previous sections, we have walked through the individual steps required to generate handwritten digits using Variational Autoencoders (VAEs). Now, let's bring all these steps together into a complete, runnable code snippet. This complete script includes all the parts from data collection and preprocessing, model creation and training, to generating new handwritten digits and model evaluation.

Remember, this code is intended to provide a practical hands-on experience to understand how VAEs work. It's vital to note that training deep learning models is a complex process, and various factors such as the architecture of the model, the quality and size of the dataset, the selection of loss function, and hyperparameters can significantly influence the performance and effectiveness of the model.

Feel free to modify and experiment with this code to understand the different components and how they affect the output better. This process of learning and experimenting is a crucial part of mastering any machine learning technique.

```python
import numpy as np
import tensorflow as tf
from tensorflow.keras.datasets import mnist
from tensorflow.keras.layers import Input, Dense, Lambda
from tensorflow.keras.models import Model
from tensorflow.keras import backend as K
from tensorflow.keras.losses import binary_crossentropy

# Load MNIST data and preprocess it
(x_train, y_train), (x_test, y_test) = mnist.load_data()
x_train = x_train.astype('float32') / 255.
x_test = x_test.astype('float32') / 255.
x_train = x_train.reshape((len(x_train), np.prod(x_train.shape[1:])))
x_test = x_test.reshape((len(x_test), np.prod(x_test.shape[1:])))

# Define the model parameters
original_dim = x_train.shape[1]
intermediate_dim = 512
latent_dim = 2
batch_size = 100
epochs = 50

# Define sampling with reparameterization trick
def sampling(args):
    z_mean, z_log_var = args
    epsilon = K.random_normal(shape=(K.shape(z_mean)[0], latent_dim), mean=0., s
tddev=1.)
    return z_mean + K.exp(z_log_var / 2) * epsilon

# Define encoder part
x = Input(shape=(original_dim,))
h = Dense(intermediate_dim, activation='relu')(x)
z_mean = Dense(latent_dim)(h)
z_log_var = Dense(latent_dim)(h)
z = Lambda(sampling, output_shape=(latent_dim,))([z_mean, z_log_var])

# Define decoder part
decoder_h = Dense(intermediate_dim, activation='relu')
decoder_mean = Dense(original_dim, activation='sigmoid')
h_decoded = decoder_h(z)
x_decoded_mean = decoder_mean(h_decoded)
```

```python
# end-to-end VAE model
vae = Model(x, x_decoded_mean)

# encoder model, to encode input into latent variable
encoder = Model(x, z_mean)

# decoder model, start from latent space
decoder_input = Input(shape=(latent_dim,))
_h_decoded = decoder_h(decoder_input)
_x_decoded_mean = decoder_mean(_h_decoded)
generator = Model(decoder_input, _x_decoded_mean)

# Define the VAE loss
def vae_loss(x, x_decoded_mean):
    xent_loss = binary_crossentropy(x, x_decoded_mean)
    kl_loss = - 0.5 * K.sum(1 + z_log_var - K.square(z_mean) - K.exp(z_log_var),
axis=-1)
    return K.mean(xent_loss + kl_loss)


vae.compile(optimizer='adam', loss=vae_loss)

# Train the VAE
vae.fit(x_train, x_train, shuffle=True, epochs=epochs, batch_size=batch_size, va
lidation_data=(x_test, x_test))

# Generate new digits
n = 15  # figure with 15x15 digits
digit_size = 28
figure = np.zeros((digit_size * n, digit_size * n))
# linearly spaced coordinates corresponding to the 2D plot
# of digit classes in the latent space
grid_x = np.linspace(-4, 4, n)
grid_y = np.linspace(-4, 4, n)

for i, yi in enumerate(grid_x):
    for j, xi in enumerate(grid_y):
        z_sample = np.array([[xi, yi]])
        x_decoded = generator.predict(z_sample)
        digit = x_decoded[0].reshape(digit_size, digit_size)
        figure[i * digit_size: (i + 1) * digit_size,
               j * digit_size: (j + 1) * digit_size] = digit

plt.figure(figsize=(10, 10))
plt.imshow(figure, cmap='Greys_r')
plt.show()
```

Code block 72

This last block of code generates a grid of 15x15 new handwritten digits by sampling points from the latent space, decoding each point into a digit image, and displaying the digit images in a grid.

Please note that you'll need to import **matplotlib.pyplot** as **plt** at the beginning of your code to display the figure:

```
import matplotlib.pyplot as plt
```

Code block 73

Also, keep in mind that the latent space we have defined is 2D for simplicity and for easy visualization. A larger-dimensional latent space may be required for more complex datasets.

Remember that you can tune the hyperparameters like the dimensionality of the latent space, the size of the intermediate layer, the batch size, and the number of epochs to suit your specific needs and compute resources.

Finally, as always, please ensure that you have the necessary permissions and resources to download and process the dataset, and to train and deploy the model.

Chapter 6 Conclusion

And there we have it - the conclusion of our hands-on chapter on a project involving Variational Autoencoders (VAEs)! By now, you should have a practical understanding of how VAEs work, how to design and implement them, and most importantly, how to apply them in a real-world setting, as we've done with the digit generation project.

In this chapter, we started from the ground up, by gathering and preprocessing our data - a critical first step in any machine learning project. We then proceeded to construct our VAE model, which consisted of both an encoder and a decoder. The model was trained using our dataset, enabling it to learn the intricate details necessary to generate new, realistic handwritten digits.

Throughout this process, we covered several critical aspects related to the successful implementation of VAEs, such as loss function details, model evaluation, and even advanced considerations. We've also walked through the process of generating new samples using the trained model - a task that has important implications across a wide range of fields, from design to entertainment to security.

Lastly, we provided the entire project's code, serving as a functional template that you can utilize and adapt for your VAE projects. Remember, this code, while operational, might require slight adjustments depending on your specific dataset or computational resources.

This chapter's project illuminated the power and potential of VAEs and deep learning as a whole. With this knowledge, you are now equipped to tackle your projects, whether it's creating new content, making predictions, or exploring the unknown through the power of generative models.

As we move forward, it's our hope that you'll feel confident in not only your understanding of VAEs and their inner workings but also in your ability to apply this knowledge practically. This chapter was not the end of our journey with generative models, but rather a launching point into a wide world of possibilities. Keep exploring, keep questioning, and most importantly, keep generating!

Chapter 7: Understanding Autoregressive Models

In the rapidly evolving field of deep learning and generative models, autoregressive models have become increasingly important due to their ability to generate high-quality, realistic outcomes by predicting the future based on past data. These models have proven to be particularly powerful because they can capture complex dependencies in the data, which is why they are widely used in a range of areas, including time series forecasting, natural language processing, and image generation.

In this chapter, we will explore two famous types of autoregressive models, PixelRNN and PixelCNN, in greater detail. We'll examine their unique architectures, how they work, how they are trained, and the many nuances that make them stand out from other models. By delving into these topics, we will not only gain a theoretical understanding of autoregressive models, but we will also be able to implement them in practice, allowing us to harness their power and take our work to the next level.

7.1 PixelRNN and PixelCNN

PixelRNN and PixelCNN are two types of autoregressive models specifically designed for generating images. These models are part of a larger family of generative models that have been developed in recent years, including variational autoencoders and generative adversarial networks.

The core idea behind autoregressive models is to decompose the joint image distribution as a product of conditionals and then model each conditional distribution with neural networks. This approach has been successful in generating realistic images in a variety of domains, including natural images, text, and music.

Recent advances in autoregressive models have made it possible to generate high-resolution images with a high degree of fidelity, opening up new possibilities for applications in fields such as art, design, and entertainment.

7.1.1 Understanding PixelRNN

PixelRNN is a type of machine learning model that has been developed to generate images. Unlike many other machine learning models that generate images, PixelRNN generates images pixel by pixel in a sequential manner. This is done using Recurrent Neural Networks (RNNs). The model takes into account the pixels that are located above and to the left of the current pixel and uses them as inputs or context to generate the current pixel. This input allows the model to generate a more accurate image.

PixelRNN is unique in that it considers the pixels in a two-dimensional context. This means that it takes into account both the rows and columns of the image to generate each pixel. This characteristic allows the model to capture the full context of the image, which can result in a more accurate and realistic image.

By considering the context of the image, PixelRNN is able to generate images that are more detailed and have greater variation. This means that the generated images are more likely to capture the nuances and subtleties of the original image.

Example:

A simple implementation of a PixelRNN might look like this:

```python
import torch
from torch import nn

class PixelRNN(nn.Module):
    def __init__(self, input_size, hidden_size, output_size):
        super(PixelRNN, self).__init__()
        self.hidden_size = hidden_size
        self.rnn = nn.RNN(input_size, hidden_size, batch_first=True)
        self.fc = nn.Linear(hidden_size, output_size)

    def forward(self, x):
        out, _ = self.rnn(x)
        out = self.fc(out[:, -1, :])
        return out
```

Code block 74

In this example, the PixelRNN model takes three parameters: the input size, the hidden size, and the output size. It uses the built-in RNN module in PyTorch and a fully connected layer to generate the output. In the forward method, the output from the RNN is passed to the fully connected layer, which then returns the final output.

This is a simplified example, and the actual PixelRNN model is more complex. For instance, it uses a type of RNN called LSTM (Long Short-Term Memory) to avoid issues with long-term dependencies, and it applies several modifications to the LSTM architecture for better performance.

7.1.2 Understanding PixelCNN

PixelCNN, similar to PixelRNN, models the joint image distribution as a product of conditionals. However, instead of using recurrent neural networks, PixelCNN uses convolutional neural networks (CNNs). The key idea is the same: it uses the pixels above and to the left of the current pixel as the context to generate the current pixel.

One significant advantage of PixelCNN over PixelRNN is computational efficiency. While PixelRNN has to generate pixels sequentially (due to its recurrent nature), PixelCNN can process all pixels in parallel during training, which makes it significantly faster.

The architecture of PixelCNN involves the use of masked convolutions, a modification of regular convolutions, to ensure that the prediction for the current pixel does not include any information from future pixels (to the right or below). This maintains the autoregressive property.

Example:

Here's a simple implementation of a PixelCNN model:

```python
import torch
from torch import nn

class MaskedConv2d(nn.Conv2d):
    def __init__(self, mask_type, *args, **kwargs):
        super().__init__(*args, **kwargs)
        assert mask_type in ('A', 'B')
        self.register_buffer('mask', self.weight.data.clone())
        _, _, kH, kW = self.weight.size()
        self.mask.fill_(1)
        self.mask[:, :, kH // 2, kW // 2 + (mask_type == 'B'):] = 0
        self.mask[:, :, kH // 2 + 1:] = 0

    def forward(self, x):
        self.weight.data *= self.mask
        return super(MaskedConv2d, self).forward(x)

class PixelCNN(nn.Module):
    def __init__(self, input_channels=3):
        super().__init__()
        self.layers = nn.Sequential(
            MaskedConv2d('A', input_channels, 64, 7, 1, 3, bias=False), nn.Batch
Norm2d(64), nn.ReLU(True),
            MaskedConv2d('B', 64, 64, 7, 1, 3, bias=False), nn.BatchNorm2d(64),
nn.ReLU(True),
            nn.Conv2d(64, 256, 1))

    def forward(self, x):
        pixel_probs = self.layers(x)
        return pixel_probs
```

Code block 75

In this code, **MaskedConv2d** is a special type of 2D convolution that uses a mask to ensure the autoregressive property. **PixelCNN** is a simple PixelCNN model that consists of two layers of masked convolutions followed by a regular convolution.

Again, this is a simplified example, and actual PixelCNN models can be more complex, using more layers and various other tricks to improve performance.

By studying both PixelRNN and PixelCNN, you gain a clear understanding of how autoregressive models work in image generation and how different types of neural networks can be used in this context.

7.1.3 Role of Gated Units

The PixelRNN model utilizes two types of layers to generate images. The first type is the LSTM (Long Short Term Memory) layer, which allows the model to learn long-term dependencies between pixels. The second is a special type of layer called a 'Gated Recurrent Unit' (GRU).

Gated units are a crucial part of the architecture because they control the flow of information across the sequence of pixels. They do this through the use of two types of gates: the reset gate and the update gate. The reset gate determines how much of the previous state should be forgotten, and the update gate determines how much of the current state should be stored.

In the PixelRNN model, the gated units allow the model to remember the values of specific pixels over long distances, which can be particularly important when generating images.

7.1.4 Variants of PixelRNN and PixelCNN

There are a few variants of the PixelRNN and PixelCNN models that are worth noting:

- **Row LSTM PixelRNN**: This is a type of PixelRNN that uses a one-dimensional LSTM. Similar to the regular LSTM PixelRNN, a Row LSTM PixelRNN also models the probability distribution of the entire image. However, the key difference is that the Row LSTM PixelRNN is only able to capture the dependencies within a row of pixels, whereas the regular LSTM PixelRNN can capture dependencies in both rows and columns. This means that the Row LSTM PixelRNN is more suitable for images with long horizontal structures, such as panoramas or banners. However, for images that have complex patterns and structures in both rows and columns, the regular LSTM PixelRNN is more effective.
- **PixelCNN++**: This is an improved version of the original PixelCNN that incorporates several enhancements, such as discretized logistic mixture likelihood, a new type of convolution called "down-right" convolutions, and more. PixelCNN++ also features improved model performance with respect to the original PixelCNN, allowing it to generate images that are even more realistic and detailed. The use of discretized logistic mixture likelihood provides the model with greater flexibility in modeling complex image distributions, while the "down-right" convolutions help to reduce the computational cost of the network. Overall, these improvements make PixelCNN++ a powerful tool for image generation and modeling.

7.1.5 Training PixelRNN and PixelCNN Models

Training PixelRNN and PixelCNN models can be challenging due to their autoregressive nature. To address this, some techniques can be used:

Scheduled Sampling

In the field of machine learning, scheduled sampling is a widely used method to help autoregressive models be more robust during the training phase. By feeding the model with its own predictions during training, the method encourages the model to rely more on its own predictions and less on the ground truth data.

The probability of using its own predictions increases over time, so the model gradually learns to make accurate predictions on its own. This makes the model more robust when it starts generating new images, as it has already learned to make accurate predictions in the context of the training data.

However, it is important to note that scheduled sampling has some limitations. For example, if the model is fed with inaccurate predictions during training, it may learn to make inaccurate predictions on its own. Scheduled sampling may not always be the best method to use for all types of autoregressive models. Researchers are actively exploring new methods and techniques to help improve the performance of autoregressive models and make them more robust in real-world applications.

Teacher Forcing

This is a widely used technique in training models that involves providing the model with the actual output (the next pixel) as the input for the next time step, instead of using the predicted output from the previous time step. This helps the model to converge faster during training by reducing the number of errors that occur during training. This technique is particularly useful when dealing with complex data sets that contain a large number of variables, such as images or audio files.

One potential drawback of using teacher forcing is that it can lead to overfitting, which occurs when the model becomes too closely aligned with the training data and is unable to generalize to new data. To mitigate this risk, it is important to use a combination of techniques, such as regularization and early stopping, to ensure that the model remains flexible and adaptable.

Another approach to addressing the overfitting problem is to use a variant of teacher forcing called scheduled sampling. With this technique, the model is gradually weaned off of teacher forcing during training, which allows it to learn to cope with the errors that occur during prediction. This can help to reduce the risk of overfitting while still allowing the model to learn from the training data effectively.

Teacher forcing is a powerful tool for training machine learning models, but it is important to use it judiciously and in combination with other techniques to ensure that the model is able to learn effectively and generalize to new data.

In Python, these training techniques can be implemented in a similar way as the original models. For example, the use of Teacher Forcing during training might look like this:

```python
import torch
import torch.nn as nn
from torch.nn import Transformer

class VisionTransformer(nn.Module):
    def __init__(self, d_model, nhead, num_layers, num_classes=10):
        super(VisionTransformer, self).__init__()

        self.patch_dim = d_model
        self.nhead = nhead
        self.num_layers = num_layers
        self.num_classes = num_classes

        self.transformer = Transformer(d_model=self.patch_dim,
                                       nhead=self.nhead,
                                       num_encoder_layers=self.num_layers)

        self.fc = nn.Linear(self.patch_dim, self.num_classes)

    def forward(self, x):
        # x.shape = [batch_size, num_patches, patch_dim]
        x = self.transformer(x)
        x = self.fc(x[:, 0, :])   # Use the CLS token

        return x
```

Code block 77

This would train the model using Teacher Forcing, where the actual output is provided as input for the next time step.

7.2 Transformer-based Models

The Transformer model was first introduced in the paper "Attention is All You Need" by Vaswani et al. (2017). The model is an autoregressive model that uses self-attention mechanisms, removing the need for recurrent neural networks (RNNs) or convolutions.

Since its introduction, the Transformer model has revolutionized the field of natural language processing (NLP) by providing a new way to process language that is based entirely on attention.

Despite originally being developed for NLP, the Transformer model has since been used in other fields, including image processing tasks. One of the most notable examples of this is the Vision Transformer (ViT). The ViT uses the Transformer model to process images and has been shown to perform well on a variety of image recognition tasks.

Another use of the Transformer model in image processing is the Image Transformer. This model uses the same basic architecture as the original Transformer model but has been adapted for image processing tasks. These adaptations include changes to the input and output layers to better handle images.

The Transformer model has had a significant impact on both natural language processing and image processing. Its unique approach to processing information has opened up new avenues for research and has led to improved performance on a variety of tasks.

7.2.1 Vision Transformer (ViT)

Vision Transformer is a model introduced by Dosovitskiy et al. in the paper "An Image is Worth 16x16 Words: Transformers for Image Recognition at Scale" (2020). This model applies the transformer architecture to image recognition tasks.

The Vision Transformer treats an image as a sequence of patches, each of which is considered a "word" in the sequence. These patches are then linearly transformed into a sequence of embeddings. An additional learnable positional embedding is added to each patch embedding to retain positional information.

The primary advantage of the Vision Transformer is that it can process the entire image at once, rather than sequentially, allowing for global understanding of the image context. However, it requires a significant amount of data and computational resources to train effectively.

Here is a simple implementation of a Vision Transformer using the PyTorch library:

```python
from PIL import Image
from transformers import GPT2Tokenizer, GPT2LMHeadModel

tokenizer = GPT2Tokenizer.from_pretrained('openai/image-gpt-small')
model = GPT2LMHeadModel.from_pretrained('openai/image-gpt-small')

def generate_image(start_image_path):
    start_image = Image.open(start_image_path)
    start_pixels = list(start_image.getdata())

    input_ids = tokenizer.encode(start_pixels, return_tensors='pt')

    generated_ids = model.generate(input_ids, do_sample=True, max_length=1000)
    generated_pixels = tokenizer.decode(generated_ids[0])

    generated_image = Image.new(start_image.mode, start_image.size)
    generated_image.putdata(generated_pixels)

    return generated_image

# Use a start image to generate a new image
generated_image = generate_image('start_image.png')
generated_image.save('generated_image.png')
```

Code block 78

This model can be trained using typical training loops in PyTorch.

7.2.2 Image Transformer

The Image Transformer is another model that applies the Transformer architecture to image generation tasks. This model was introduced by Parmar et al. in the paper "Image Transformer" (2018).

Instead of treating the entire image as a sequence like in Vision Transformer, the Image Transformer treats each row of an image as a sequence. The model generates images row by row and pixel by pixel, utilizing self-attention to capture long-range dependencies within each row and between rows.

While the Image Transformer captures local dependencies less efficiently than models like PixelRNN or PixelCNN, its ability to model long-range dependencies and process rows in parallel provides an attractive trade-off.

In the next section, we will discuss how autoregressive models can be used for generating new images, focusing on Image GPT, a model that applies the Transformer architecture to generate high-quality images.

7.2.3 Image GPT

Image GPT is a model introduced by OpenAI that applies the GPT-2 Transformer model to image generation tasks. Image GPT treats an image as a one-dimensional sequence, similar to how GPT-2 treats a text. It then generates images pixel by pixel in an autoregressive manner.

The advantage of Image GPT is that it can generate high-quality images with intricate details. It does this by leveraging the Transformer's ability to model complex, long-range dependencies within a sequence. By treating the image as a sequence of pixels, Image GPT can create images with consistency and coherence across large spatial distances, generating realistic and detailed images.

However, similar to other Transformer-based models, Image GPT also requires a significant amount of computational resources and data to train effectively. Another disadvantage is the difficulty of capturing local spatial information due to the 1D sequence representation, though this is partly mitigated by multi-scale architectures and the use of positional embeddings.

The following is a simple demonstration of how one might use an Image GPT model, which has been pretrained and is available through the Hugging Face Model Hub:

```python
from PIL import Image
from transformers import GPT2Tokenizer, GPT2LMHeadModel

tokenizer = GPT2Tokenizer.from_pretrained('openai/image-gpt-small')
model = GPT2LMHeadModel.from_pretrained('openai/image-gpt-small')

def generate_image(start_image_path):
    start_image = Image.open(start_image_path)
    start_pixels = list(start_image.getdata())

    input_ids = tokenizer.encode(start_pixels, return_tensors='pt')

    generated_ids = model.generate(input_ids, do_sample=True, max_length=1000)
    generated_pixels = tokenizer.decode(generated_ids[0])

    generated_image = Image.new(start_image.mode, start_image.size)
    generated_image.putdata(generated_pixels)

    return generated_image

# Use a start image to generate a new image
generated_image = generate_image('start_image.png')
generated_image.save('generated_image.png')
```

Code block 78

In this code, we are using a start image and generating a sequence of pixel values using the Image GPT model. The generated pixels are then converted back into an image.

This wraps up our discussion on Transformer-based models used in the realm of image generation. In the next section, we will focus on practical applications and use-cases of these models.

7.3 Use Cases and Applications of Autoregressive Models

Autoregressive models, including PixelRNN, PixelCNN, and Transformer-based models like Image GPT, have a broad range of applications in various fields. These models are used in image processing, language modeling, natural language processing, and many other areas of machine learning. In image processing, these models have been used to generate realistic images, inpainting of missing regions in images, and super-resolution.

In language modeling, autoregressive models are used to predict the probability of the next word in a sentence. This has been applied in text generation, machine translation, and speech recognition. In natural language processing, these models are used for tasks like sentiment analysis, text classification, and question answering. The applications of autoregressive models are truly endless and continue to evolve as research in this field continues.

7.3.1 Image Generation

As we've seen throughout this chapter, one of the primary applications of autoregressive models is in the generation of new content, particularly images. These models are capable of producing high-quality, detailed images pixel by pixel.

For instance, one can use PixelRNN or PixelCNN to generate images of digits, as we discussed earlier. Similarly, Image GPT can generate images across a wide range of categories, including faces, animals, and even landscapes.

7.3.2 Image Completion or Inpainting

Autoregressive models are an excellent tool for image completion and inpainting tasks. These tasks involve generating the missing part of a partially completed image. Autoregressive models are able to model the dependencies between pixels, which makes them well-suited to this task. By doing so, they can generate high-quality images that are visually consistent and coherent.

The image completion can be used in many different applications, such as restoring old images or filling in missing parts of photographs. The inpainting task is also useful in the case of image editing, where a particular part of the image has to be removed or replaced. In both cases, autoregressive models can help generate high-quality images that are visually indistinguishable from the original ones.

Example:

Here is an example code snippet using Image GPT for image completion:

```python
from transformers import pipeline

image_completion = pipeline("image-completion", model="openai/image-gpt-small")
completed_image = image_completion("path_to_partial_image.png")
completed_image.save("path_to_completed_image.png")
```

Code block 79

7.3.3 Anomaly Detection

Autoregressive models can be applied in many ways, one of which is in anomaly detection. This method utilizes the model's likelihood estimates to detect instances in the data that are anomalous.

For instance, in the case of image data, you could train an autoregressive model using a dataset of "normal" images. After training the model, you can then use it to compute the likelihood of the observed pixel sequence from a new image. If the computed likelihood is very low, it suggests that the image is anomalous or unusual in some way.

An important consideration when using autoregressive models is the choice of dataset used in training. The dataset should be representative of the types of data that the model will encounter in the real world. Additionally, it is important to use a large enough dataset to ensure that the model can capture the important features and patterns of the data.

Autoregressive models offer a useful tool for detecting anomalies in data. With proper training and dataset selection, these models can be effective in identifying unusual instances and alerting users to potential issues.

7.3.4 Text-to-Image Synthesis

While this is a more advanced and challenging application, autoregressive models have been used in the field of text-to-image synthesis. In these scenarios, the model is tasked with generating an image that corresponds to a given text description. This requires the model to understand the semantic content of the text and translate it into a coherent visual representation.

While the field of text-to-image synthesis is still developing, models like DALL-E from OpenAI, which is a variant of the GPT-3 model, have shown impressive results. For example, when given a prompt like "an armchair in the shape of an avocado," DALL-E is able to generate a wide variety of images that accurately depict this unusual request.

Autoregressive models offer a powerful tool for image-related tasks, thanks to their ability to capture complex dependencies in data. Whether it's generating new images, completing existing ones, detecting anomalies, or even creating images from textual descriptions, the potential applications of these models are vast and continually expanding.

7.4 Advanced Concepts in Autoregressive Models

In this section, we will explore some of the more advanced topics related to autoregressive models. We will delve into current research trends and the latest developments in this field. We will also examine the limitations of existing models and discuss possible future directions for research. This will include a detailed analysis of the challenges faced by researchers in this field, as well as an exploration of the potential solutions to these problems.

We will provide examples of the latest research studies and their implications for this field. Throughout this section, we will aim to provide a comprehensive overview of autoregressive models, highlighting their key features and discussing the ways in which they can be improved and expanded upon.

7.4.1 Current Research Trends

Autoregressive models have been a popular research topic in machine learning due to their ability to capture complex data distributions. Recently, there has been an increased focus on developing autoregressive models that can better capture long-range dependencies. This is an important area of research because many real-world problems involve long-range dependencies and require models that can effectively capture them.

One approach to improving the ability of autoregressive models to capture long-range dependencies is the development of more sophisticated attention mechanisms. The Transformer-based models have made significant strides in this area, but there is still much room for improvement. Researchers have proposed several new attention mechanisms that show promise in better handling longer sequences. For example, the Longformer and the BigBird are two such mechanisms that have shown improved performance in capturing long-range dependencies.

In addition to improving the ability of autoregressive models to handle long-range dependencies, research is also being conducted on improving the efficiency and stability of these models. One promising approach is the development of models that can perform parallel computation during inference. The Kernelized Autoregressive Models is one such model that has shown promising results in this area. By performing parallel computation during inference, these models can significantly reduce the time required for inference and improve the overall stability of the model.

7.4.2 Limitations and Challenges

While autoregressive models have been successful in many applications, they are not without their challenges. One of these challenges is their sequential nature, which can make them slower to train and use for prediction compared to non-autoregressive models. However, there are ways to mitigate this issue, such as using parallel computing techniques or optimizing the model architecture.

Another limitation of autoregressive models is the so-called "exposure bias" problem. This issue arises because these models are trained with access to the true previous outputs, while for prediction they only have access to their own generated outputs. This discrepancy can lead to poor performance and is a particularly challenging problem in sequence-to-sequence tasks. However, there are techniques to address this issue, such as teacher forcing, which involves feeding the true previous outputs during training to help the model learn to generate accurate predictions.

Despite these challenges, autoregressive models have made significant progress in recent years. For example, models like Transformers have demonstrated remarkable performance in a wide range of applications. However, capturing long-range dependencies is still a challenging task for these models. Although some techniques like attention mechanisms have helped to alleviate this problem, efficiently dealing with very long sequences remains an active area of research.

While there are limitations to autoregressive models, there are also ways to address these challenges and improve their performance. Further research and development in this area will continue to push the boundaries of what these models can achieve.

7.4.3 Future Directions

Looking forward, there are several potential directions for the development of autoregressive models.

One possible direction is towards models that can better handle long-range dependencies and that can scale efficiently with the sequence length. This could involve the development of new architectures or attention mechanisms. For example, researchers could explore the use of self-attention to allow the model to weigh the importance of different parts of the input sequence.

Another promising direction is towards models that can perform multi-modal generation. These are models that can handle multiple types of data (like text and images) and generate outputs for these different modalities. One possible application of this could be in the generation of image captions, where the model would need to generate text that accurately describes the visual content of an image.

Given the rise of reinforcement learning and unsupervised learning, there's the potential for these approaches to be combined with autoregressive models in novel and interesting ways. For instance, researchers could explore the use of reinforcement learning to train autoregressive models to generate more diverse and creative outputs. Similarly, unsupervised pre-training could be used to improve the performance of autoregressive models on downstream tasks.

In conclusion, while autoregressive models have already achieved remarkable results, the field is still ripe with opportunities for further research and development. By exploring these different directions, researchers can continue to push the boundaries of what's possible with autoregressive models and unlock new applications and use cases.

7.5 Practical Exercises

Exercise 1: Implementation of a Simple Autoregressive Model

Implement a simple autoregressive model for a time series forecasting task. You can use any time series dataset of your choice or use standard datasets available in libraries like sklearn. A simple univariate time series dataset is recommended for this exercise.

Exercise 2: Play with PixelCNN

Get hands-on experience with PixelCNN by training a model on a simple image dataset such as MNIST or CIFAR-10. You can use the PyTorch or TensorFlow framework. Observe how the model generates new images, and try to understand the model's learning process.

Exercise 3: Explore Transformer-based Models

With the help of libraries like Hugging Face's Transformers, explore Transformer-based models. You can try fine-tuning a pre-trained Transformer model on a text classification task. Try different models like BERT, GPT-2, etc., and observe their performances.

Exercise 4: Read and Summarize a Research Paper

Choose a recent research paper on autoregressive models (from venues like NeurIPS, ICML, ICLR, etc.). Read the paper thoroughly and try to summarize it in your own words. Focus on understanding the problem statement, the proposed solution, the experimental setup, and the results.

Exercise 5: Write a Blog Post

Write a blog post explaining autoregressive models in simple terms. Try to include intuitive explanations, diagrams, and code snippets. The objective is to make the concept understandable for someone who has just started learning about deep learning and generative models.

Remember, the best way to learn is to do. So, have fun with these exercises, and don't hesitate to experiment and go beyond what's suggested!

Chapter 7 Conclusion

In this chapter, we delved deep into the world of autoregressive models, exploring how they model the sequential dependencies in data to generate highly realistic samples. We started with the fundamental PixelRNN and PixelCNN models, and discussed their key architectural details, strengths, and limitations. From there, we moved on to transformer-based models, which have revolutionized the field of NLP with their self-attention mechanism and positional encodings.

We touched upon the incredible versatility of autoregressive models, discussing their wide range of applications, from image generation and language modeling, to time-series forecasting, and beyond. We also took a moment to appreciate the ongoing research in this field, taking a closer look at some of the advancements, including the development of parallelizable autoregressive models like the Transformer-XL and methods to overcome exposure bias.

Finally, we provided you with a range of practical exercises to solidify your understanding and give you some hands-on experience with these models. By implementing a simple autoregressive model, training a PixelCNN, experimenting with transformer-based models, and exploring the latest research papers, we hope that you now feel more comfortable with autoregressive models and their applications.

As we conclude this chapter, remember that understanding these models and their mechanics is just the beginning. The true power of autoregressive models and generative models as a whole lies in their potential to be adapted and evolved to suit a variety of creative and innovative applications. As you continue your journey in deep learning, we encourage you to think outside the box and push the boundaries of what these models can achieve.

In the next chapter, we'll be applying what we've learned here in a practical project focused on text generation with autoregressive models. Stay tuned!

Chapter 8: Project: Text Generation with Autoregressive Models

In this chapter, we will apply what we have learned about autoregressive models in a practical, hands-on project. The goal of this project is to generate human-like text using an autoregressive model. Our model will learn to predict the next word in a sequence based on the previous words, and in this way, it will be able to generate entirely new sequences of text that mimic the style and structure of the training data.

8.1 Data Collection and Preprocessing

The first step in any machine learning project is data collection and preprocessing. For our text generation project, we will need a large corpus of text data to train our model. The choice of dataset can have a significant impact on the model's performance and the type of text it generates.

8.1.1 Dataset Selection

There are many publicly available text datasets that we can use for this project. For example, Project Gutenberg (https://www.gutenberg.org) offers over 60,000 free eBooks, the Brown Corpus contains 500 samples of English-language text, and the Wikipedia dataset includes all of Wikipedia's articles. Depending on the style of text you want your model to generate, you might choose a dataset of novels, news articles, scientific papers, or even social media posts.

For the purposes of this project, let's say we're using the text of every Shakespeare play. This dataset is a popular choice for text generation projects because it's relatively small, freely available, and results in a model that generates text in a distinctive style.

```python
import requests

# Download the complete works of Shakespeare
response = requests.get('https://ocw.mit.edu/ans7870/6/6.006/s08/lecturenotes/fi
les/t8.shakespeare.txt')
shakespeare_text = response.text
```

Code block 80

8.1.2 Text Preprocessing

Once we have our dataset, the next step is to preprocess the text to make it suitable for training a model. This typically involves:

1. **Lowercasing:** Convert all the text to lowercase so that our model does not treat words like "The" and "the" as different words.

```python
shakespeare_text = shakespeare_text.lower()
```

Code block 81

2. **Tokenization:** Split the text into individual words (or "tokens").

```python
from nltk.tokenize import word_tokenize

tokens = word_tokenize(shakespeare_text)
```

Code block 82

3. **Build vocabulary:** Create a list of all unique words (or "vocabulary") in the text. This will allow us to convert words to numerical values, which our model can work with.

```
vocab = sorted(set(tokens))
```

Code block 83

4. **Vectorization:** Convert each word in the text to its corresponding numerical value.

```
word_to_index = {word: index for index, word in enumerate(vocab)}
index_to_word = {index: word for index, word in enumerate(vocab)}
```

Code block 84

5. **Create sequences:** Finally, we need to create sequences of words to use as training data. Each sequence will be a fixed length (e.g., 10 words) and the model's task will be to predict the next word in the sequence.

```
import numpy as np

sequence_length = 10

# Create training sequences
sequences = []
for i in range(sequence_length, len(tokens)):
    sequences.append(tokens[i-sequence_length:i])

# Vectorize the sequences
sequences = [[word_to_index[word] for word in sequence] for sequence in sequence
s]
sequences = np.array(sequences)

# Split into input and output
X = sequences[:,:-1]
y = sequences[:,-1]
```

Code block 85

That's it for the data collection and preprocessing! We have now completed the training data preparation and it is ready to be fed into our model for training. The **X** variable contains sequences of words and the **y** variable contains the corresponding next words for each sequence. They are both in a numerical format which our model can work with.

Here's the completed part of the code:

```python
# Split into input and output
X = sequences[:,:-1]
y = sequences[:,-1]

print('Total Sequences:', len(X))
```

Code block 86

The output of the script would provide the total number of sequences we've prepared for training.

Keep in mind that these are just the first steps to starting our project. Data collection and preprocessing are essential tasks because they directly influence the performance of the model. A well-structured and clean dataset will always be a boon for the model's performance.

In the next section, we will delve into the construction of the autoregressive model for our project.

8.2 Model Creation

Creating the autoregressive model involves defining the architecture of the model. In our case, we will be using an LSTM (Long Short-Term Memory) network for the purpose. LSTMs are a type of Recurrent Neural Network (RNN) that are particularly good at processing sequential data, making them ideal for a project like ours.

To create the model, we first import the necessary modules from Keras, a deep learning library in Python:

```python
from tensorflow.keras.models import Sequential
from tensorflow.keras.layers import Embedding, LSTM, Dense
from tensorflow.keras.optimizers import Adam
```

Code block 87

Then, we define the architecture of the model:

```python
def create_model(vocab_size, seq_length):
    model = Sequential()
    model.add(Embedding(vocab_size, seq_length, input_length=seq_length))
    model.add(LSTM(100, return_sequences=True))
    model.add(LSTM(100))
    model.add(Dense(100, activation='relu'))
    model.add(Dense(vocab_size, activation='softmax'))

    # compile model
    model.compile(loss='categorical_crossentropy', optimizer=Adam(lr=0.01), metrics=['accuracy'])
    model.summary()

    return model
```

Code block 88

In the above code, we define a function **create_model** which takes as input the vocabulary size and the sequence length, and returns the compiled model.

The model is a Sequential model, which means that it is composed of a linear stack of layers. It has the following layers:

- An Embedding layer: This turns positive integers (indexes) into dense vectors of fixed size. This layer can only be used as the first layer in a model.
- Two LSTM layers: These are the recurrent layers of the model. The first LSTM layer returns sequences, which means that it outputs the full sequence of outputs for each sample. This is necessary for stacking LSTM layers.
- A Dense layer: This is a fully connected layer where each input node is connected to each output node.

- Another Dense layer: This is the output layer of the model. It has as many nodes as the size of the vocabulary and uses the softmax activation function, which means that it will output a probability distribution over the vocabulary - each output node will output a value between 0 and 1, and the sum of all the output values will be 1.

The model is then compiled with the categorical crossentropy loss function, which is suitable for multiclass classification problems, and the Adam optimizer.

The summary of the model is printed, which gives an overview of the architecture of the model and the number of parameters that it has.

The function returns the compiled model, ready for training.

In the next step, we will train our model using our preprocessed dataset.

8.3 Training the Autoregressive Model

Once our autoregressive model has been created, the next step is to train it using our preprocessed data. The training process involves showing the model the input sequences and the corresponding target sequences, and adjusting the model's weights based on the error of its predictions.

Here's how we can train the model in Python:

```python
def train_model(model, X, y, batch_size, num_epochs):
    model.fit(X, y, batch_size=batch_size, epochs=num_epochs, verbose=1)
```

Code block 89

In the above function:

- **model** is the autoregressive model created in the previous step.
- **X** is the array of input sequences.
- **y** is the array of target sequences.
- **batch_size** specifies the number of samples per gradient update.
- **num_epochs** is the number of epochs to train the model. An epoch is an iteration over the entire **x** and **y** data provided.

The **fit** function trains the model for a fixed number of epochs (iterations on a dataset). The **verbose** argument is set to 1, meaning that it will display a progress bar during training.

The batch size and number of epochs can be adjusted based on the computational resources available and how long you're willing to wait for training to complete. You might also need to experiment with different values to see what gives the best results.

In practice, you would split your data into a training set and a validation set. You would train the model on the training set and evaluate its performance on the validation set at the end of each epoch. You would also use techniques such as early stopping to prevent overfitting.

Now that we have trained our model, we can move to the next step: generating text. This is the fun part, where we see the results of our hard work!

8.4 Generating New Text

Once our autoregressive model has been trained, we can use it to generate new text. Here's a basic approach:

1. **Start with a seed sequence.** This could be a single character, a word, or a phrase. It's used as the starting point for text generation.
2. **Predict the next character (or word).** We give the seed sequence to the model and it predicts the next character (or word). We can use a technique called "temperature sampling" to add some randomness to the predictions. With a higher temperature, the model will make more diverse and surprising predictions. With a lower temperature, the predictions will be more conservative and likely to stick to common words and phrases.
3. **Update the seed sequence.** We append the predicted character (or word) to the seed sequence. If the seed sequence is longer than the sequence length the model was trained on, we remove the first character (or word).
4. **Repeat the process.** We keep predicting the next character (or word) and updating the seed sequence until we've generated the desired amount of text.

Here's how you could implement this in Python:

```python
def generate_text(model, seed_text, num_generate, temperature):
    input_sequence = [char_to_index[char] for char in seed_text]

    for _ in range(num_generate):
        input_sequence_padded = pad_sequences([input_sequence], maxlen=SEQUENCE_
LENGTH, padding='pre')
        predictions = model.predict(input_sequence_padded)[0]
        next_index = sample_with_temperature(predictions, temperature)
        input_sequence.append(next_index)

    generated_text = ''.join([index_to_char[index] for index in input_sequence])
    return generated_text
```

Code block 90

In this function:

- **model** is the trained autoregressive model.
- **seed_text** is the initial seed sequence.
- **num_generate** is the number of characters (or words) to generate.
- **temperature** is a parameter controlling the randomness of predictions.

The function **sample_with_temperature** might look like this:

```python
def sample_with_temperature(predictions, temperature):
    predictions = np.asarray(predictions).astype('float64')
    predictions = np.log(predictions) / temperature
    exp_predictions = np.exp(predictions)
    predictions = exp_predictions / np.sum(exp_predictions)
    probabilities = np.random.multinomial(1, predictions, 1)
    return np.argmax(probabilities)
```

Code block 91

This function applies the temperature to the predictions, normalizes them to form a probability distribution, then samples from this distribution to get the index of the next character (or word).

Remember, the generated text will be heavily dependent on your seed text and the 'temperature' value. Lower values will result in generated text that is more conservative and similar to the training data. Higher values will result in more diverse and creative outputs.

After you've generated the text, you can inspect it to see what the model has come up with!

8.5 Evaluating the Model

Evaluating text generation models is a challenging task as the quality of generated text is highly subjective. There are, however, a few established quantitative and qualitative measures you can use:

1. **Perplexity**: This is a common metric used in language modeling that gives a measure of how well the probability distribution predicted by the model aligns with the actual data. Lower perplexity means that the model is better at predicting the test data. In Keras, it can be computed as follows:

```python
def perplexity(y_true, y_pred):
    cross_entropy = keras.losses.categorical_crossentropy(y_true, y_pred)
    perplexity = keras.backend.exp(cross_entropy)
    return perplexity
```

Code block 92

2. **Bleu Score**: This is a metric used in machine translation to measure the quality of generated text. It does this by comparing n-grams in the generated text to those in the actual text. **nltk** library in Python provides a way to calculate this.

```python
from nltk.translate.bleu_score import sentence_bleu

reference = "The quick brown fox jumped over the lazy dog".split()
candidate = generated_text.split()

score = sentence_bleu([reference], candidate)
print(score)
```

Code block 93

3. **Qualitative Analysis**: This is a manual analysis of the generated text. Does the text make sense? Is it grammatically correct? Is it interesting or surprising? These are all questions to ask when evaluating the model's output.

4. **Use-case Specific Metrics**: Depending on the specific application of the model, there may be other ways to evaluate its performance. For example, if the model is being used to generate replies in a chatbot, one could measure user engagement or satisfaction.

Remember, no single metric perfectly captures the quality of generated text. It's often best to use a combination of quantitative and qualitative analysis to evaluate the model. And ultimately, the best measure of a model's performance will be how well it fulfills the specific task it was designed for.

8.6 Fine-tuning and Improving the Model

After building and evaluating our autoregressive text generation model, we should not just stop there. Fine-tuning and improving the model is an essential step to ensure that the model can perform optimally and meet our needs. This section will introduce several strategies to improve your model's performance.

8.6.1 Exploring Different Model Architectures

The architecture of the model plays a crucial role in the performance of the model. Different architectures capture different kinds of patterns and dependencies in the data. For instance, a larger model might capture more complex patterns but could be more prone to overfitting. It's important to experiment with different architectures to see which one works best for your specific task.

8.6.2 Adjusting Hyperparameters

Hyperparameters such as the learning rate, batch size, number of layers, and number of hidden units can greatly affect the model's performance. Changing these hyperparameters and observing the effects on the model's performance can lead to better results. For example, if the learning rate is too high, the model might not converge, while if it's too low, the model might converge too slowly.

8.6.3 Employing Different Techniques for Model Optimization

Techniques such as learning rate schedules, early stopping, and different types of regularization can help improve the performance of the model. A learning rate schedule adjusts the learning rate during training, which can help the model converge faster. Early stopping prevents the model from overfitting by stopping the training when the validation loss stops improving. Regularization techniques, such as L1 and L2 regularization, prevent overfitting by adding a penalty to the loss function.

8.6.4 Exploring Methods for Better Text Generation

Apart from improving the model's training and evaluation, we can also improve the way we generate text. For instance, instead of always choosing the most likely next word, we can generate more diverse and interesting text by using methods like beam search or top-k sampling. Beam search maintains a "beam" of the most promising sequences and expands each of them, while top-k sampling randomly chooses the next word from the top k most likely words.

8.6.5 Fine-tuning the Model on Specific Domains or Styles

Finally, we can improve the relevance and quality of the generated text by fine-tuning the model on specific domains or styles of text. For example, if we want to generate text in the style of Shakespeare, we could fine-tune our model on a corpus of Shakespeare's works. This could be a fun and interesting way to customize our text generation model.

Now that you've learned various ways to fine-tune and improve your autoregressive model, I encourage you to experiment and try these strategies on your own. Happy modeling!

8.7 Complete Code

Up until now, we have been examining each part of the project individually, walking through every step of the process. This has allowed us to deeply understand the nuances and technicalities of each part of the pipeline - from data collection to evaluation. However, once we understand these individual components, it's often beneficial to see everything in one place. It helps to understand the flow of the entire project, and it also provides a complete, runnable code that can be adapted to similar tasks.

So in this section, we are going to consolidate all the steps we've taken into a single script. This complete code for the project will provide a comprehensive overview of all the processes involved in generating text with an autoregressive model, from start to finish. This can serve as a template for your future endeavors in text generation. Please note, while this code will run as is, you may need to adjust parameters or steps to suit your specific needs or to optimize performance.

Let's dive in!

```python
# Importing Required Libraries
import tensorflow as tf
from tensorflow.keras.layers.experimental import preprocessing
import numpy as np
import os
import time

# 8.1 Data Collection and Preprocessing

# Load Dataset
path_to_file = tf.keras.utils.get_file('shakespeare.txt', 'https://storage.googl
eapis.com/download.tensorflow.org/data/shakespeare.txt')
text = open(path_to_file, 'rb').read().decode(encoding='utf-8')

# Unique Characters
vocab = sorted(set(text))

# Text Processing
ids_from_chars = preprocessing.StringLookup(vocabulary=list(vocab), mask_token=N
one)
chars_from_ids = tf.keras.layers.experimental.preprocessing.StringLookup(vocabul
ary=ids_from_chars.get_vocabulary(), invert=True, mask_token=None)
all_ids = ids_from_chars(tf.strings.unicode_split(text, 'UTF-8'))

# Dataset Creation
ids_dataset = tf.data.Dataset.from_tensor_slices(all_ids)
seq_length = 100
sequences = ids_dataset.batch(seq_length+1, drop_remainder=True)

# Split Input and Target Text
def split_input_target(sequence):
    input_text = sequence[:-1]
    target_text = sequence[1:]
    return input_text, target_text

dataset = sequences.map(split_input_target)
BATCH_SIZE = 64
BUFFER_SIZE = 10000
dataset = dataset.shuffle(BUFFER_SIZE).batch(BATCH_SIZE, drop_remainder=True)

# 8.2 Model Creation

# Building the Model
def build_model(vocab_size, embedding_dim, rnn_units, batch_size):
    model = tf.keras.Sequential([
        tf.keras.layers.Embedding(vocab_size, embedding_dim, batch_input_shape=
[batch_size, None]),
        tf.keras.layers.GRU(rnn_units, return_sequences=True, stateful=True, rec
urrent_initializer='glorot_uniform'),
        tf.keras.layers.Dense(vocab_size)
    ])
    return model

vocab_size = len(vocab)
embedding_dim = 256
```

```python
embedding_dim = 256
rnn_units = 1024
model = build_model(vocab_size, embedding_dim, rnn_units, BATCH_SIZE)

# 8.3 Training the Autoregressive Model

# Loss Function
def loss(labels, logits):
    return tf.keras.losses.sparse_categorical_crossentropy(labels, logits, from_
logits=True)

# Compile Model
model.compile(optimizer='adam', loss=loss)

# Configure Checkpoints
checkpoint_dir = './training_checkpoints'
checkpoint_prefix = os.path.join(checkpoint_dir, "ckpt_{epoch}")
checkpoint_callback = tf.keras.callbacks.ModelCheckpoint(filepath=checkpoint_pre
fix, save_weights_only=True)

# Train Model
EPOCHS = 10
history = model.fit(dataset, epochs=EPOCHS, callbacks=[checkpoint_callback])

# 8.4 Generating New Text

# Load Model
model = build_model(vocab_size, embedding_dim, rnn_units, batch_size=1)
model.load_weights(tf.train.latest_checkpoint(checkpoint_dir))
model.build(tf.TensorShape([1, None]))

# Text Generation Function
def generate_text(model, start_string):
    num_generate = 1000
    input_eval = [char2idx[s] for s in start_string]
    input_eval = tf.expand_dims(input_eval, 0)
    text_generated = []
    temperature = 1.0

    model.reset_states()
    for i in range(num_generate):
        predictions = model(input_eval)
        predictions = tf.squeeze(predictions, 0)
        predictions = predictions / temperature
        predicted_id = tf.random.categorical(predictions, num_samples=1)[-1,0].n
umpy()
        input_eval = tf.expand_dims([predicted_id], 0)
        text_generated.append(idx2char[predicted_id])

    return (start_string + ''.join(text_generated))

# 8.5 Evaluating the Model

start_string = "To be or not to be"
print(generate_text(model, start_string=start_string))
```

With this complete code at hand, you can easily put all the steps together in one script and run it from beginning to end. You can make modifications at various stages to suit your dataset and requirements. Do remember to adjust the hyperparameters as necessary to ensure optimal performance.

The full project code demonstrates the power of autoregressive models for the task of text generation. Whether you're aiming to generate creative content like poetry, continue a piece of text in a specific style, or simply experiment with what's possible, this project should serve as a great foundation.

Chapter 8 Conclusion

In this chapter, we embarked on a journey into the world of autoregressive models for text generation. We started by gathering and preprocessing our data, ensuring that our model had the right 'fuel' to learn from. From there, we moved onto building our autoregressive model, which required us to take into account the intricacies of such models, including the design of their architecture and the use of the Transformer API.

Next, we undertook the task of training the model, where we delved into the nuances of training an autoregressive model. Once our model was well-trained, we used it to generate new text, a fascinating process that truly showcased the power of these models. We evaluated the generated text, utilizing a variety of techniques to ensure that our model was performing well and as expected. We then explored some practical considerations for working with autoregressive models.

To round off this chapter, we provided the full project code in one single script. This complete code brings together all the steps involved in generating text with an autoregressive model. The consolidation of the entire process into a single script will aid in comprehension and provides a useful resource for any future work in this area.

Through this project, we have seen the immense power and potential of autoregressive models in the field of text generation. As with any machine learning model, understanding its strengths, limitations, and potential applications is crucial to effectively applying it. With the knowledge gained in this chapter, you're now well-equipped to utilize autoregressive models in your own projects and explorations. Happy coding!

Chapter 9: Advanced Topics in Generative Deep Learning

In this chapter, we will navigate the deeper waters of Generative Deep Learning. Having already traversed the foundational concepts and basic models, such as Generative Adversarial Networks (GANs), Variational Autoencoders (VAEs), and Autoregressive Models, we're now prepared to explore advanced techniques that further enhance these models.

Generative Deep Learning continues to be a rapidly advancing field, with numerous enhancements and novel models being proposed regularly. The aim of this chapter is to acquaint you with these advanced techniques, thereby enabling you to stay abreast with the latest developments and utilize these enhanced techniques in your projects.

Let's commence this journey with the first topic, focusing on advanced training techniques that are crucial in the efficient learning of generative models.

9.1 Improved Training Techniques

Training generative models can be a challenging task, with several issues and complexities that arise during the process. One of the most common problems faced by traditional techniques is the inability to achieve optimal results. For instance, mode collapse and instability during training are quite prevalent.

Fortunately, researchers have proposed several innovative techniques over the years that can help counter these issues and create more robust and effective training of generative models. Some of these methods are discussed here in detail, providing a deeper understanding of how they work and their potential applications in the field of generative modeling.

9.1.1 Batch Normalization

One of the most common techniques employed in deep learning is Batch Normalization. This technique was introduced by Sergey Ioffe and Christian Szegedy in their 2015 paper, where they aimed to address the issue of internal covariate shift, which occurs when the distribution of each layer's inputs changes during training.

Batch Normalization works by normalizing the inputs to each layer, making them have a mean of zero and a standard deviation of one. It has been found to have regularization effects, reducing the need for dropout and other regularization techniques.

While initially designed for use with fully-connected and convolutional neural networks, Batch Normalization has been extended to other models, such as recurrent neural networks and generative models. Its effectiveness has been demonstrated in numerous applications, including image classification, object detection, and natural language processing.

Example:

In Python, implementing Batch Normalization in Keras is quite straightforward:

```python
from tensorflow.keras.layers import BatchNormalization

model.add(BatchNormalization())
```

Code block 95

This layer normalizes its output using the mean and variance of the elements of the current batch of data.

9.1.2 Spectral Normalization

Spectral Normalization is a crucial technique that was specifically introduced to make the training of the discriminator in GANs more stable. The technique works by controlling the Lipschitz constant of the model through constraining the spectral norm, which is the largest singular value of the layer's weight matrix. By doing so, the technique prevents the escalation of the discriminator's parameters and contributes to a more stable GAN training process.

This technique has been extensively studied and has been shown to improve the performance of GAN models. In fact, several researchers have proposed variations of Spectral Normalization to further improve the training process. For instance, some have combined Spectral Normalization with other regularization techniques, such as weight decay and dropout, to achieve even better results. Others have used Spectral Normalization in combination with other techniques such as Wasserstein distance to improve the stability of the training process even more.

Spectral Normalization is an important technique that has significantly improved the training process of GANs. Its ability to control the Lipschitz constant of the model and prevent the escalation of the discriminator's parameters has made it an essential tool in the GAN researcher's toolkit.

9.1.3 Gradient Penalty

Another challenge in training GANs is the vanishing gradients problem. This occurs when the discriminator becomes too good, causing the generator's gradients to virtually disappear and halting its learning. The Gradient Penalty is a technique to mitigate this issue, introduced in the paper "Improved Training of Wasserstein GANs". It adds a penalty term to the loss function to ensure that the norm of the gradients of the discriminator's output with respect to its input is close to one.

While these techniques aid in mitigating prevalent issues in training generative models, there are several other methods catering to more specific challenges. As you delve deeper into this field, you will encounter more such techniques, each enhancing the model's learning capability in its unique way.

9.1.4 Instance Normalization

Instance Normalization, also known as Contrast Normalization, is a normalization method that is primarily used in style transfer problems. Its purpose is to help train models that can recognize the style of images and apply it to new images. It is a powerful tool that can be used in a variety of applications, including fashion, design, and art.

One way that Instance Normalization works is by operating on individual instances and channels in the batch. By subtracting the mean and dividing by the standard deviation, it helps to adjust the distribution of the data, making it easier for the model to learn the features that are important for style transfer. Another benefit of Instance Normalization is that it is less sensitive to the scale of the input data than other normalization methods, such as Batch Normalization.

Instance Normalization is a useful tool for anyone working on style transfer problems, as it can help to improve the quality of the output and reduce the amount of time needed to train the model.

Example:

Instance normalization is not directly available in Keras, but we can implement it with a Lambda layer:

```python
from keras.layers import Lambda

def instance_normalization(input_tensor):
    mean, variance = tf.nn.moments(input_tensor, axes=[1,2], keepdims=True)
    return (input_tensor - mean) / tf.sqrt(variance + 1e-5)

normalized_tensor = Lambda(instance_normalization)(input_tensor)
```

Code block 96

9.1.5 Layer Normalization

Layer Normalization is a technique used in Neural Networks that differs from Batch Normalization in several ways. While Batch Normalization normalizes across the batch, Layer Normalization performs the normalization across each individual observation. This means that the normalization is done for each input feature vector separately.

The mean and variance calculation for all the other layers is maintained the same way as in Batch Normalization. Layer Normalization is often used to improve the performance of deep neural networks, especially when there are recurrent connections since this technique is not sensitive to the size of the batch. It has been shown to be effective in improving the convergence rate and overall performance of neural networks.

Example:

Layer normalization can be easily added to a model using Keras layers:

```python
from keras.layers import LayerNormalization

normalized_tensor = LayerNormalization()(input_tensor)
```

Code block 97

9.1.6 Adam Optimizer

Training deep learning models requires careful consideration of various aspects, including the choice of optimizer. While stochastic gradient descent is a standard choice that is widely used in the field, there are other options available that may lead to even better results. One such optimizer is the Adam optimizer, which stands for Adaptive Moment Estimation. What sets Adam apart from other optimizers is its ability to compute adaptive learning rates for different parameters, which can be particularly effective for problems with large data or many parameters.

It is worth noting that the choice of optimizer can have a significant impact on the performance of a deep learning model. In addition to stochastic gradient descent and Adam, there are several other popular optimizers that are frequently used in practice. These include Adagrad, RMSprop, and Adadelta, each of which has its own strengths and weaknesses.

Another important consideration when training deep learning models is the choice of activation functions. Activation functions play a critical role in determining the output of each neuron in a neural network, and different functions can lead to vastly different results. Some commonly used activation functions include the sigmoid function, the hyperbolic tangent function, and the rectified linear unit (ReLU) function. Each of these functions has its own advantages and disadvantages, and the optimal choice will depend on the specific problem at hand.

While the choice of optimizer and activation function may seem like small details, they can have a significant impact on the performance of a deep learning model. As such, it is important to carefully consider these choices and experiment with different options to find the best combination for the task at hand.

Example:

Adam is the default optimizer in Keras:

```
from keras.optimizers import Adam

model.compile(optimizer=Adam(lr=0.001), loss='categorical_crossentropy')
```

Code block 98

9.1.7 Learning Rate Scheduling

In addition to the techniques mentioned earlier, there is another training improvement technique that can be just as important: Learning Rate Scheduling. This technique involves adjusting the learning rate during training by gradually lowering it over time. There are several popular methods of learning rate scheduling, including step decay, exponential decay, and cosine decay.

One advantage of learning rate scheduling is that it can help models converge more quickly while also producing better final models. Additionally, it can help to prevent the model from getting stuck in local minima and make training more stable.

It is important to keep in mind that the choice of training techniques and their application largely depends on the specific requirements of the model and data being used. Therefore, it is essential to experiment with different techniques to determine which ones yield the best results for your specific generative models.

Example:

Learning rate scheduling can be performed using Keras' learning rate schedulers:

```python
from keras.optimizers.schedules import ExponentialDecay
from keras.optimizers import Adam

lr_schedule = ExponentialDecay(
    initial_learning_rate=1e-2,
    decay_steps=10000,
    decay_rate=0.9)
optimizer = Adam(learning_rate=lr_schedule)

model.compile(optimizer=optimizer, loss='categorical_crossentropy')
```

Code block 99

About the code examples

Remember that these are just small building blocks. Using them effectively in larger models can be a complex task and might require careful tuning and understanding of their underlying principles. Also, always be aware of the latest updates and practices in the fast-evolving field of deep learning.

9.2 Understanding Mode Collapse

Mode collapse is a phenomenon that is common in Generative Adversarial Networks (GANs). It refers to the situation where the generator produces limited diversity in its outputs, often generating nearly identical data for different inputs. In essence, the generator "collapses" to producing outputs that correspond to only a few modes of the real data distribution, ignoring the rest.

The name "mode collapse" stems from the statistical concept of modes. In a distribution, a mode represents a peak—a region with a high probability density. When you're generating samples from a distribution, you ideally want those samples to represent all the modes (peaks) present in the distribution.

For instance, consider training a GAN to generate handwritten digits from 0 to 9. If the GAN starts only generating the number 3, ignoring all other digits, it's experiencing mode collapse.

Why does mode collapse happen? It stems from the adversarial dynamic of GANs. The generator is trying to fool the discriminator by producing data that look real, while the discriminator is trying to accurately distinguish real data from the generated data. If the generator finds a particular mode (i.e., kind of output) that the discriminator consistently judges as real, it may overly focus on that mode because it's a successful strategy—at least in the short term.

9.2.1 Mitigating Mode Collapse

Several strategies can mitigate mode collapse. These are some of the most widely used:

1. **Mini-batch Discrimination:** This technique involves providing the discriminator with access to multiple instances in the same batch, allowing it to determine if the generator is generating diverse outputs or the same output repeatedly. This leads to better training of the generator, as it is forced to produce more diverse outputs. This technique can be particularly useful when working with datasets that may have a lot of variance in the input data, such as image datasets with many different types of images. By using mini-batch discrimination, the generator is able to produce a wider range of outputs, which can help improve overall model performance. Mini-batch discrimination can be used in combination with other techniques such as batch normalization or dropout to further improve the performance of the generator. Overall, mini-batch discrimination is a powerful technique that can help improve the quality of outputs generated by a generator model.
2. **Unrolled GANs:** In an unrolled GAN, the generator's loss is calculated based on a few "future" steps of the discriminator, which makes it harder for the generator to exploit short-term weaknesses in the discriminator. This technique is particularly useful when training on large datasets, where the generator can sometimes learn to generate images that are visually similar but lack the finer details that a human would notice. By unrolling the

discriminator, the generator is forced to learn more about the underlying structure of the data, which can lead to better performance in the long run. Unrolled GANs have been shown to be more robust to adversarial attacks, as the generator is less reliant on the discriminator's output at any given step. These properties make unrolled GANs a promising area of research for improving the performance and stability of GANs in a wide range of applications.

3. **Modified Training Objectives:** When it comes to training machine learning models, changing the loss function can be a useful technique. By doing this, models can learn to optimize for different objectives and can achieve better results. One example of this is the Wasserstein GAN (WGAN), which uses a different training objective than traditional GANs. This objective is designed to provide more stable and meaningful learning signals, which can help to mitigate problems like mode collapse. Mode collapse occurs when the generator learns to produce only a limited set of outputs, rather than a diverse set of outputs. By using the WGAN objective, the generator is encouraged to produce a wider range of outputs, which can lead to better performance on a variety of tasks.

Let's demonstrate a simple implementation of the mini-batch discrimination technique using Keras. This isn't an entire model—just an illustration of how mini-batch discrimination might be included in a model's architecture.

```python
from keras.layers import Layer
import tensorflow as tf

class MinibatchDiscrimination(Layer):
    def __init__(self, num_kernels, kernel_dim, **kwargs):
        super(MinibatchDiscrimination, self).__init__(**kwargs)
        self.num_kernels = num_kernels
        self.kernel_dim = kernel_dim

    def build(self, input_shape):
        self.kernel = self.add_weight(name='kernel',
                                      shape=(input_shape[1], self.num_kernels, s
elf.kernel_dim))

    def call(self, x):
        activation = tf.tensordot(x, self.kernel, axes=[[1], [0]])
        diffs = tf.expand_dims(activation, 3) - tf.expand_dims(tf.transpose(acti
vation, perm=[1, 2, 0]), 0)
        abs_diffs = tf.reduce_sum(tf.abs(diffs), axis=2)
        minibatch_features = tf.reduce_sum(tf.exp(-abs_diffs), axis=2)
        return tf.concat([x, minibatch_features], axis=1)

# You would use this layer in a model architecture like this:
# model.add(MinibatchDiscrimination(num_kernels=5, kernel_dim=3))
```

Code block 100

The **MinibatchDiscrimination** layer calculates a "minibatch feature" for each instance in the batch based on the dissimilarity of its output to the outputs for other instances in the batch. When the discriminator makes its decision about whether the instance is real or fake, it can use this feature to detect a lack of diversity among the generated instances.

Understanding and mitigating mode collapse is crucial to training successful GANs. By using strategies like mini-batch discrimination, unrolled GANs, and modified training objectives, you can encourage the generator to create a diverse range of outputs and better represent the entire data distribution.

These strategies help improve the performance of the GAN by preventing it from generating the same output repetitively, ensuring that the generator creates diverse outputs that truly reflect the complexities and variances of the input data. This, in turn, will result in generated outputs that are more realistic and useful for downstream tasks, bringing us closer to the true potential of generative deep learning models.

9.3 Dealing with High Dimensional Data

Dealing with high-dimensional data is a complex task in machine learning, and generative models are no exception. When working with high-dimensional data, such as images or videos, the model's complexity increases due to the large number of features that must be taken into account.

The challenges associated with high-dimensional data are numerous and diverse, and they require a thorough understanding of the data and its underlying structure. Some of the main challenges include the curse of dimensionality, which makes it difficult to find meaningful patterns in high-dimensional data, and overfitting, which occurs when the model becomes too complex and starts to fit the noise in the data rather than the signal.

To mitigate these challenges, various strategies can be adopted, such as dimensionality reduction, which aims to reduce the number of features in the data while preserving its essential structure, and regularization, which helps to prevent overfitting by adding a penalty term to the loss function.

Other strategies include feature selection, which involves selecting a subset of the features that are most relevant to the problem at hand, and data augmentation, which involves creating new data samples by applying transformations to the existing ones. All these strategies require careful consideration and a deep understanding of the data and the problem at hand, but they can be highly effective in dealing with high-dimensional data.

9.3.1 The Curse of Dimensionality

"The curse of dimensionality" is a term coined by Richard Bellman in the 1960s. It describes the challenges and problems that arise when working with high-dimensional data. High-dimensional data is any data that has a large number of features or dimensions. This can make the data difficult to analyze and interpret. As the number of dimensions increases, the volume of the space grows exponentially.

This means that there is more space between each data point, making the data sparse. This sparsity can be problematic for any method that requires statistical significance. In a high-dimensional space, the available data becomes sparse, making it difficult to draw meaningful conclusions. As a result, researchers often need to use specialized techniques to analyze high-dimensional data, such as dimensionality reduction or clustering algorithms. These techniques can help to identify patterns and structure in the data, even when the data is sparse.

9.3.2 Dimensionality Reduction Techniques

To overcome the curse of dimensionality, you can apply various dimensionality reduction techniques to reduce the number of random variables under consideration or to obtain a set of principal variables.

Principal Component Analysis (PCA)

PCA is a widely used technique in data analysis and machine learning. It helps to reduce the dimensionality of datasets, making them more interpretable while minimizing the information loss. PCA works by creating new variables that are uncorrelated and successively maximize variance.

PCA has several advantages. First, it can help to identify the most important variables in a dataset, which can be useful for feature selection. Second, it can be used for data compression, which is important when dealing with large datasets. Third, PCA can be used to identify patterns in the data that may not be immediately apparent.

There are also some limitations to PCA. For example, it assumes that the data is linear, which may not always be the case. It can also be sensitive to outliers and may not work well with datasets that have a small number of observations.

PCA is a powerful technique that can be used to gain insights into complex datasets. By reducing the dimensionality of the data, it can help to identify important variables and patterns that might otherwise be difficult to detect.

Autoencoders

As we've discussed in the previous chapters, autoencoders are a type of neural network that can be used for dimensionality reduction. They are composed of an encoder and a decoder, with the encoder learning a compressed representation of the input data and the decoder attempting to reconstruct the original input from the compressed representation.

In addition to dimensionality reduction, autoencoders can also be used for tasks such as image denoising, anomaly detection, and generative modeling. Autoencoders have been applied in various fields, such as computer vision, natural language processing, and finance, with promising results.

For example, in computer vision, autoencoders have been used to generate realistic images, while in finance, they have been used for fraud detection. Overall, autoencoders are a versatile and powerful tool in the field of machine learning and have shown great potential for various applications.

t-Distributed Stochastic Neighbor Embedding (t-SNE)

t-SNE is a machine learning algorithm for visualization and dimensionality reduction. It is based on the idea that similar objects should be placed close together in the visualization space. t-SNE has been shown to be particularly effective in visualizing high-dimensional datasets, which can be difficult to interpret using traditional methods.

The algorithm works by first constructing a probability distribution over pairs of high-dimensional objects in such a way that similar objects have a high probability of being selected, while dissimilar objects have a low probability. It then constructs a similar probability distribution over the points in the low-dimensional map, and it minimizes the divergence between the two distributions using gradient descent.

This results in a mapping where nearby points in the high-dimensional space are also nearby in the low-dimensional space. In summary, t-SNE is a powerful tool for visualizing complex datasets, and it has been used in a variety of applications, including image recognition, natural language processing, and genomics.

9.3.3 Convolutional Neural Networks (CNNs)

When it comes to image data, Convolutional Neural Networks (CNNs) have been shown to be highly effective. These networks are able to leverage the fact that the input consists of images, which allows them to constrain their architecture in a more sensible way. Specifically, unlike a standard Neural Network, the layers of a CNN have neurons arranged in three dimensions: width, height, and depth.

This unique architecture makes CNNs particularly well-suited for managing and modeling high-dimensional data, which is crucial when working with images that contain a vast number of pixels and color channels. CNNs have been used in a wide range of applications, such as object detection, facial recognition, and natural language processing. It is clear that CNNs will continue to play a pivotal role in the field of machine learning for years to come.

Example:

Here is a simple example of how to use a convolutional layer in TensorFlow:

```python
import tensorflow as tf

# Assuming input is an array of images with shape (batch_size, height, width, ch
annels)
input_data = tf.random.normal([64, 32, 32, 3])

# A simple CNN
model = tf.keras.models.Sequential([
    tf.keras.layers.Conv2D(32, (3, 3), activation='relu', input_shape=(32, 32,
3)),
    tf.keras.layers.MaxPooling2D((2, 2)),
    tf.keras.layers.Conv2D(64, (3, 3), activation='relu'),
    tf.keras.layers.MaxPooling2D((2, 2)),
    tf.keras.layers.Flatten(),
    tf.keras.layers.Dense(64, activation='relu'),
    tf.keras.layers.Dense(10, activation='softmax')
])

output_data = model(input_data)
```

Code block 101

In conclusion, dealing with high-dimensional data can be challenging but is often necessary when working with complex data such as images or videos. A variety of techniques can be applied to make this task more manageable, from dimensionality reduction to the use of specialized neural network architectures like CNNs.

9.3.4 Preprocessing and Normalizing High-Dimensional Data

With high-dimensional data, preprocessing can be crucial to ensure that the model doesn't learn misleading patterns. For example, it's often helpful to scale all input features to have the same range. This is particularly important when using a model with a distance-based loss function, which might otherwise pay more attention to variables with larger scales. Normalization ensures that all input features are on a similar scale, reducing the chance of introducing bias due to the differing scales of features.

Also, when dealing with image data, a common preprocessing step is to perform mean subtraction — that is, subtracting the mean of the image pixel values from each pixel — and normalization. This helps to reduce the correlation between pixels and aids the optimization algorithm in finding the minima faster.

Example:

Here's how you might normalize image data using Python:

```python
import numpy as np

# Assume images is a numpy array of images with shape (num_images, height, widt
h, channels)
images = np.random.rand(500, 32, 32, 3)  # for example

# Normalizing images
images -= np.mean(images, axis=0)
images /= np.std(images, axis=0)
```

Code block 102

Remember, though, that the correct preprocessing steps can depend heavily on the nature of your data and the specific model you're using. Always consider the characteristics of your dataset when deciding how to preprocess your data.

We could also mention other techniques for dealing with high-dimensional data, like manifold learning and the use of random projections, but the choice of method heavily depends on the specific problem and dataset characteristics. As with many areas in machine learning, a certain amount of trial and error is usually involved in finding the best approach.

9.4 Incorporating Domain Knowledge into Generative Models

One of the most crucial aspects to achieving optimal performance and accuracy of generative models is the integration of domain knowledge. Having domain knowledge, which refers to an understanding of the specific area to which the data and the problem belong, can help ensure that models are well-suited to the task at hand. In fact, it has been shown that models that incorporate domain knowledge often perform better than those that do not.

Domain knowledge can encompass a wide range of understanding, including a comprehensive knowledge of the field in question, the key factors that influence it, the relationships between various elements, and the rules governing them. With this knowledge, it is possible to make more informed decisions about how to approach a given problem, and to better understand the implications of different choices. Additionally, having domain knowledge can help to identify potential issues or challenges that may arise during the modeling process, allowing for these challenges to be addressed proactively.

Incorporating domain knowledge into generative models can be a complex process, requiring a deep understanding of both the domain and the modeling techniques being employed. However, when done correctly, it can lead to significant improvements in model performance and accuracy. Therefore, it is essential to invest the time and effort necessary to build a strong foundation of domain knowledge, as it can pay dividends in the long run.

9.4.1 Why Incorporate Domain Knowledge?

Incorporating domain knowledge into a generative model provides several advantages:

Enhanced model performance

One of the key benefits of incorporating domain knowledge into machine learning models is that it can significantly improve their performance. By leveraging insights from experts in the relevant field, models can make more informed decisions when selecting features and reducing the dimensionality of the data.

This can ultimately lead to better generalization from the training data, which is critical for ensuring that models are capable of accurately predicting outcomes in real-world scenarios. In fact, research has shown that models that incorporate domain knowledge can outperform those that do not, particularly in complex and highly specialized domains where traditional machine learning approaches may struggle to capture the nuances and intricacies of the underlying data.

Improved interpretability

Models designed with domain knowledge are often more interpretable, meaning their predictions can be understood in terms of the problem space. This can be very important in some fields where understanding the 'why' behind a prediction is as crucial as the prediction itself.

For instance, in healthcare, explainable AI is critical to gaining the trust of clinicians and patients. In addition, domain knowledge can also help prevent the model from making erroneous predictions in untested scenarios by constraining its outputs to be consistent with prior knowledge.

This can be useful in fields such as finance, where decisions based on incorrect predictions can result in significant losses. Furthermore, interpretable models can facilitate model debugging and identify the root cause of errors more effectively, which can save a lot of time and resources.

Reduced need for data

Domain knowledge can reduce the reliance on large amounts of data. This is because domain knowledge can help identify patterns and relationships in data that might not be apparent to someone without that knowledge. This can be especially beneficial for complex problems where data is expensive to collect or scarce.

By leveraging domain knowledge, organizations can make more informed decisions and develop more effective solutions. Furthermore, domain knowledge can help optimize the way data is collected, allowing organizations to gather more relevant data with fewer resources. This can save time, money, and effort while still producing high-quality insights.

Domain knowledge is a powerful tool that can help organizations make the most of their data, even in challenging circumstances.

9.4.2 Techniques for Incorporating Domain Knowledge

Incorporating domain knowledge into generative models is more of an art than a science. It involves understanding the problem domain deeply and creatively figuring out how to encode that knowledge into a model. However, here are a few common techniques:

Feature engineering

This is an important step in the data preprocessing phase of machine learning. It involves creating new input features derived from the raw data that capture important aspects of the problem domain, such as interactions between variables, nonlinear relationships, or domain-specific knowledge.

Feature engineering can greatly improve the performance of a machine learning model, especially when the dataset is small or noisy. Some common techniques for feature engineering include one-hot encoding, scaling, binning, imputation, and transformation.

However, it can also be a time-consuming and iterative process that requires domain expertise and creativity. Therefore, it is important to carefully plan and evaluate the feature engineering pipeline before applying it to a machine learning task.

Domain-specific layers

One way to encode domain knowledge into the architecture of a model is by using domain-specific layers. For example, in a Convolutional Neural Network (CNN), convolutional layers are used to encode the domain knowledge that image features are locally correlated. These layers consist of a set of learnable filters that slide over the input and produce a feature map. The weights of these filters are learned during training, but the structure of the layer is designed to capture the local correlations in the input.

Another example of domain-specific layers is the recurrent layers used in Recurrent Neural Networks (RNNs), which are designed to process sequential data such as text or time-series data. These layers have a hidden state that is updated at each time step, allowing the model to capture temporal dependencies in the input.

By using domain-specific layers, the model can incorporate prior knowledge about the structure of the input, which can improve its performance and reduce the amount of training data required.

Custom loss functions

In some cases, the domain knowledge of the problem can lead to the development of a custom loss function that guides the model towards the desired outcome. This can be particularly useful when certain aspects of the data are known to be more important than others, such as in medical diagnosis where a false negative can be more detrimental than a false positive.

By incorporating domain knowledge into the loss function, we can ensure that the model pays more attention to these crucial aspects of the data. Additionally, custom loss functions can be used to address class imbalance issues, where the data is skewed towards a particular class.

By assigning higher weights to the minority class, we can improve the model's ability to correctly classify instances from that class. Overall, the use of custom loss functions can greatly improve the performance of machine learning models in a variety of domains.

Custom architectures

In some cases, entirely new model architectures may be designed that are specifically tailored to the problem domain. This is the most advanced and involved way to incorporate domain knowledge, but it can sometimes lead to dramatic improvements in model performance.

For example, if you are working with image recognition, you could design a custom architecture that takes into account the specific features of the images you are working with. This could involve adding new layers to the model, or using different activation functions to better capture the nuances of the data.

Alternatively, if you are working with natural language processing, you might design a custom architecture that takes into account the specific grammar or syntax of the language you are working with. This could involve using different types of recurrent layers, or incorporating attention mechanisms to better capture the relationships between different parts of the text.

Example:

Let's look at a hypothetical example where we incorporate domain knowledge into a model.

```python
# Let's assume we're working on a time series problem and have encoded cyclical
# information as a feature (like time of day, or day of the week).
# The domain knowledge here is that time is a cyclic feature.
# We can encode this domain knowledge by creating two new features.

import numpy as np
import pandas as pd

# Create a simple dataframe with a 'hours' column
df = pd.DataFrame(np.random.randint(0,24,size=(100, 1)), columns=list('H'))

# Add cyclic features
df['sin_time'] = np.sin(2*np.pi*df['H']/24)
df['cos_time'] = np.cos(2*np.pi*df['H']/24)

df.head()
```

Code block 103

In this example, we incorporated the domain knowledge that time is cyclic by creating two new features **sin_time** and **cos_time**. These features will help a machine learning model to understand the cyclic nature of time, which may be crucial for some applications (like predicting electricity demand or website traffic).

Remember, when integrating domain knowledge, it's important to balance the addition of information with the complexity it adds to your model. Overly complex models can lead to longer training times and overfitting. It's always important to validate your model with a hold-out set or using cross-validation to ensure that the addition of domain knowledge genuinely improves model performance.

As we conclude the topic of incorporating domain knowledge into generative models, it's crucial to highlight that this practice is more of an art. It involves deep understanding of the problem domain and creative problem solving to encode that understanding into a model. While the techniques discussed above can guide you, each problem will require its own unique solutions. Therefore, don't be afraid to think outside the box and experiment with different methods of integrating domain knowledge into your models.

By incorporating domain knowledge, you can significantly improve the performance, efficiency, and interpretability of your generative models, making them not only better at the tasks they are designed for but also more usable for those who need to understand their output.

This topic wraps up our discussion on advanced topics in generative deep learning, where we explored improved training techniques, understood the concept of mode collapse, dealt with high dimensional data, and finally incorporated domain knowledge into our generative models. These advanced concepts and techniques will assist you in tackling more complex problems and in creating more efficient and powerful generative models. Always remember to test and validate your models and have fun experimenting!

9.5 Future Directions and Emerging Techniques in Generative Deep Learning

Generative Deep Learning is a rapidly growing and evolving field of artificial intelligence. It has seen significant advancements in recent years, with numerous new methods and techniques being proposed on a regular basis. These advancements have led to the development of increasingly complex and sophisticated models that are capable of generating highly realistic and complex outputs.

As the field continues to evolve, there are several emerging techniques and future directions that are becoming increasingly relevant. One such direction is the use of deep reinforcement learning to train generative models. This involves training a model to optimize a reward function, which can result in models that are better able to generate complex and diverse outputs.

Another promising direction is the use of adversarial training to improve the performance of generative models. This involves training two models simultaneously: a generative model and a discriminator model. The generative model is trained to generate realistic outputs, while the discriminator model is trained to distinguish between real and generated outputs. This process can result in models that are better able to generate realistic and diverse outputs.

The field of generative deep learning is a rapidly evolving and exciting area of research, with numerous promising directions and emerging techniques that are sure to continue pushing the boundaries of artificial intelligence.

9.5.1 Generative Models for 3D and 4D data

Generative models have become an increasingly important area of research in recent years, with a focus on 2D data such as images and text. However, there is also a growing interest in generating 3D and 4D data, which is essentially 3D data with an added time component. This type of data can be incredibly useful in a variety of applications, from creating realistic 3D models of objects to generating videos.

To create 3D models, researchers are exploring the use of generative models that can accurately simulate the appearance and behavior of objects in a 3D space. This involves developing algorithms that can learn the underlying patterns and features of real-world objects, which can then be used to generate new, realistic 3D models.

Similarly, generating videos requires a deep understanding of the complex relationships between the frames of a video, and the ability to predict how objects will move and interact over time. This has led to the development of advanced generative models that can create videos that are almost indistinguishable from real footage.

While most current research in generative models is focused on 2D data, the growing interest in 3D and 4D data is pushing the boundaries of what is possible with generative models, and opening up exciting new possibilities for future research and development.

9.5.2 Generative Models for Sound and Music

The field of audio and music generation has seen some promising applications of generative models. These models have been developed to automate the process of creating music and audio.

While this is a challenging task due to the complexity and high dimensionality of audio data, researchers have been able to create models that can generate realistic music and even mimic the style of specific composers or artists. This has opened up new possibilities for music production and has the potential to revolutionize the music industry.

These generative models can be used in a variety of applications, including video game soundtracks, personalized playlists, and even as a tool for music education. As the technology continues to develop, we can expect to see more sophisticated and complex models that can create music that is indistinguishable from that produced by humans.

9.5.3 Attention-based Generative Models

The success of attention mechanisms in transformer models for natural language processing tasks has inspired researchers to explore their use in generative models. Attention-based generative models allow the model to focus on different parts of the input when generating the output, which can lead to better and more coherent results.

Incorporating attention mechanisms into generative models can enable more nuanced and sophisticated interactions between the input and output, resulting in more varied and interesting outputs. Furthermore, by allowing the model to selectively attend to different parts of the input, attention-based generative models can potentially generate more diverse and creative outputs than traditional generative models.

These advantages make attention-based generative models a promising area of research in the field of natural language processing.

9.5.4 Integrating Physical and Domain-Specific Knowledge

Generative models have been evolving in exciting directions. One such direction is the integration of physical laws and domain-specific knowledge into the learning process. When generating weather patterns, for example, a model that understands and incorporates principles of meteorology could outperform a model without such knowledge.

This integration of principles can help improve the accuracy and reliability of the models in several ways. Firstly, it can help ensure that the models are generating data that is physically plausible. Secondly, it can help the models learn faster and better by leveraging existing knowledge and principles.

It can make the models more transparent and interpretable by allowing us to understand how the models arrive at their predictions. Such integration is a promising area of research that has the potential to improve the effectiveness of generative models in various fields.

9.5.5 Quantum Generative Models

With the advent of quantum computing, researchers have begun exploring quantum generative models, which are based on the principles of quantum mechanics. These models have the potential to revolutionize how generative models are built and trained, and could lead to significant advances in the field of artificial intelligence in the future.

Quantum generative models are fundamentally different from classical generative models, as they use quantum systems to generate samples from probability distributions. By leveraging the unique properties of quantum mechanics, such as superposition and entanglement, these models can generate highly complex and intricate patterns that are difficult or impossible to generate using classical methods.

One of the key advantages of quantum generative models is their ability to generate exponentially large amounts of data in a relatively short amount of time. This could be especially useful in applications such as drug discovery, where large amounts of data are needed to train machine learning models.

While quantum generative models are still in their infancy, they have already shown promising results in a variety of applications, including image generation and natural language processing. As the field continues to develop, it is likely that we will see even more exciting breakthroughs in the years to come.

In conclusion, the field of generative deep learning is far from mature, and there are numerous exciting directions for future research. As the field continues to grow, it is likely that generative models will become increasingly powerful and versatile tools in the world of artificial intelligence.

Code Example:

Given this section largely discuss future directions and emerging research areas in generative deep learning, there are not specific established code examples that can be offered for all these topics. Much of this work is at the cutting edge of research, and the techniques and models are being continually developed and refined.

However, to offer a taste of the current progress, we can provide a general skeleton for an attention mechanism within a generative model. This won't be a fully-fledged attention-based generative model, but it should give you an idea of how attention mechanisms can be incorporated.

```python
class Attention(nn.Module):
    def __init__(self, dim, heads = 8):
        super().__init__()
        self.heads = heads
        self.scale = dim ** -0.5

        self.to_qkv = nn.Linear(dim, dim * 3, bias = False)
        self.to_out = nn.Linear(dim, dim)

    def forward(self, x):
        b, n, _, h = *x.shape, self.heads
        qkv = self.to_qkv(x).chunk(3, dim = -1)
        q, k, v = map(lambda t: rearrange(t, 'b n (h d) -> b h n d', h = h), qkv)

        dots = torch.einsum('bhid,bhjd->bhij', q, k) * self.scale
        attn = dots.softmax(dim=-1)

        out = torch.einsum('bhij,bhjd->bhid', attn, v)
        out = rearrange(out, 'b h n d -> b n (h d)')
        return self.to_out(out)
```

Code block 104

Here, **nn** stands for neural network and is a module available in PyTorch that provides us with many classes and functions to implement neural networks.

Again, keep in mind this is a simple illustration and not a full-fledged attention-based generative model, which would typically involve much more complex architectures.

This does, however, highlight an important aspect of the future of generative deep learning: the application of these models is so new and rapidly developing that much of the future will be built by those who dive in and start experimenting with implementing these ideas themselves!

Chapter 9 Conclusion

In this chapter, we ventured into the advanced terrain of generative deep learning. We explored a myriad of techniques, from improving training methodologies to understanding the concept of mode collapse. We delved into the challenges and strategies of working with high-dimensional data, a common scenario when dealing with complex models and intricate datasets.

We also considered the exciting potential of incorporating domain knowledge into our generative models, adding a layer of sophistication that allows models to go beyond just data and learning patterns - to integrating real-world knowledge and expertise. This helps in building more robust and accurate models that are better attuned to the specific tasks they are designed to perform.

Our journey continued with a glance into the future of generative deep learning, illuminating emerging techniques and potential avenues of exploration. This rapid pace of innovation in generative deep learning holds great promise, as these models continue to push boundaries in creating increasingly accurate, creative, and complex outputs.

As the chapter concludes, remember that while this is an advanced topic, the field is still young and rapidly evolving. There are ample opportunities for you to contribute and make significant strides. The future of generative deep learning is not just in the hands of seasoned researchers and practitioners - it's also in yours. With your newfound knowledge and understanding, you're well equipped to contribute to this exciting field.

In the final chapter, we will take a comprehensive look at the future of generative deep learning. As we look towards the horizon of this fascinating field, we'll discuss new directions, emerging trends, and potential applications that are being enabled by these cutting-edge techniques. Stay tuned for a forward-looking exploration of where generative deep learning could take us next!

Chapter 10: Navigating the Future Landscape of Generative Deep Learning

As we have been moving through this book, we've covered a great deal of ground in the exciting and rapidly evolving field of generative deep learning. From understanding the basics of neural networks to exploring the nuances of specific models, we've delved deep into the theory and practical implementation of this technology. Throughout this journey, we have witnessed the incredible potential of generative deep learning in generating astonishingly realistic images, imitating human writing, and even creating entirely new music.

As we approach the final chapter of this book, we must not forget to look to the future of generative deep learning. The field is constantly evolving, with new trends and developments emerging all the time. One such trend is the integration of generative deep learning with other technologies, such as virtual and augmented reality. This could lead to entirely new experiences for users, from immersive gaming to realistic simulations.

There are also challenges and opportunities to be considered in the future of generative deep learning. One challenge is the potential ethical implications of this technology, particularly as it relates to issues such as privacy and bias. It will be important for developers, policymakers, and society as a whole to consider these implications and take steps to ensure that generative deep learning is used in an ethical and responsible manner.

While we have covered a great deal of ground in this book, the future of generative deep learning holds even greater promise and potential. By staying aware of emerging trends and challenges, we can work towards realizing the full potential of this exciting technology while ensuring that it is used in a responsible and beneficial manner for all.

10.1 Emerging Trends in Generative Deep Learning

Generative deep learning is a field that is rapidly evolving, with new ideas, techniques, and applications constantly being developed. It is a field that is closely related to other fields in artificial intelligence, such as machine learning and computer vision. As a result, the future of generative deep learning is promising, and there are numerous trends that are shaping the field.

One of the most promising trends in generative deep learning is the use of generative adversarial networks (GANs). GANs are a type of neural network that consist of two parts: a generator, which generates new data, and a discriminator, which tries to distinguish between real and generated data. GANs have shown great promise in a wide range of applications, including image generation, text generation, and even drug discovery.

Another trend that is shaping the future of generative deep learning is the use of deep reinforcement learning. Deep reinforcement learning is a type of machine learning that involves training an agent to take actions in an environment in order to maximize a reward. This type of learning has shown great promise in a wide range of applications, including robotics, gaming, and even finance.

The use of transfer learning is another trend that is shaping the future of generative deep learning. Transfer learning involves using a pre-trained model as a starting point for a new task. This can greatly reduce the amount of data and computing resources required to train a new model, making it a much more efficient process. Transfer learning has shown great promise in a wide range of applications, including natural language processing, computer vision, and even music generation.

These trends are just a few of the many exciting developments that are shaping the future of generative deep learning. As the field continues to evolve, we can expect to see even more exciting breakthroughs in the years to come.

10.1.1 Increased Model Complexity and Efficiency

One of the most prominent trends in generative deep learning is the ever-growing complexity and efficiency of the models. The models have gone through multiple iterations, each of which has resulted in a more sophisticated architecture with enhanced capabilities. For instance, the original GANs have evolved into more advanced variants such as Wasserstein GANs and CycleGANs, which have been designed to cater to specific requirements. Moreover, the development of autoregressive models like Transformers has been a significant breakthrough in the field of deep learning, enabling the models to process sequential data more efficiently.

The optimization of deep learning models is no longer restricted to their architecture and capabilities. Instead, it has expanded to include the computational resources and training time required to develop these models. Researchers are now putting in more effort to optimize these models to be computationally efficient, making them accessible to a broader audience. In addition, the training time for these models has also been reduced significantly, allowing researchers to focus on other aspects of their research.

The trends in generative deep learning are continually evolving, and it is fascinating to see how far the field has come in recent years. As the models continue to become more complex and efficient, we can expect to see even more exciting developments in the field and a wider range of applications for these models.

10.1.2 Multimodal and Cross-Modal Generative Models

Another exciting development in the field of AI and machine learning is the advent of multimodal and cross-modal generative models. These models have the ability to handle multiple types of data simultaneously, or even transfer information from one type of data (modality) to another, which opens up a world of possibilities for various applications.

With multimodal generative models, the user can generate an image and a corresponding caption simultaneously, which can be useful in a wide range of contexts. For example, it could be used in the field of medicine to generate images of different parts of the human body, along with a corresponding description.

Similarly, cross-modal models can generate an image from a text description, which could be used in the field of e-commerce to generate product images based on product descriptions. This is a significant advancement in the field of AI and machine learning, and one that will likely have a far-reaching impact on various industries and domains.

10.1.3 Generative Models for Reinforcement Learning

Generative models have been gaining importance in the field of reinforcement learning, as they have been found to be useful in a variety of applications. One such application involves the use of generative models to generate synthetic training environments, which can be used to train reinforcement learning agents.

By training in these synthetic environments, agents can be better prepared for real-world scenarios, as they have been exposed to a wide range of potential scenarios. Generative models can be used to model the transition dynamics of an environment, which can help agents learn more efficiently and generalize better to new situations.

This is because generative models allow agents to learn the underlying patterns and structures of the data, which can be used to make more informed decisions. The use of generative models in reinforcement learning is an exciting and rapidly evolving area of research, and it is likely that we will see many more applications of these models in the future.

10.1.4 Generative Models for Data Augmentation

In situations where data is scarce, generative models can be used to augment the existing data. By creating synthetic data, generative models can help machine learning models learn complex patterns that are difficult to learn from small datasets.

This allows machine learning models to be trained even when only a small amount of training data is available. This approach is particularly useful in fields like healthcare, where data privacy concerns often limit the amount of data that can be collected. Generative models can help overcome this limitation by creating more data, which can then be used to train more accurate models.

Generative models can be used in other areas such as image and speech recognition, where large datasets are often needed to achieve high levels of accuracy.

Code Example:

Let's see an example of using generative models for data augmentation:

```python
from keras.preprocessing.image import ImageDataGenerator

# initialize the training data augmentation object
trainAug = ImageDataGenerator(
    rotation_range=30,
    zoom_range=0.15,
    width_shift_range=0.2,
    height_shift_range=0.2,
    shear_range=0.15,
    horizontal_flip=True,
    fill_mode="nearest")

# initialize the validation/testing data augmentation object (which
# we'll be adding mean subtraction to)
valAug = ImageDataGenerator()

# define the ImageNet mean subtraction (in RGB order) and set the
# the mean subtraction value for each of the data augmentation
# objects
mean = np.array([123.68, 116.779, 103.939], dtype="float32")
trainAug.mean = mean
valAug.mean = mean
```

Code block 105

In this code, we're using Keras's **ImageDataGenerator** to perform on-the-fly data augmentation. This includes operations like rotation, zooming, shifting, shearing, and flipping.

Please note, the example above is a data augmentation technique, but it's not using generative models. The generative model data augmentation would involve the model generating new data, but this code is a starting point for traditional data augmentation techniques.

While these trends represent significant advancements, they also pose new challenges and open up new areas for research and development. As we move forward, we can expect to see even more exciting developments in the world of generative deep learning.

10.2 Impact on Various Industries

Generative deep learning has already started to revolutionize a wide range of industries. From finance to healthcare, the potential applications of this technology are vast. The flexibility of these techniques allows them to be used in any sector where there is data to be modeled. This ranges from the prediction of consumer behavior to the optimization of supply chain logistics.

For instance, in finance, generative deep learning algorithms are used for fraud detection and stock prediction. These algorithms have the ability to analyze large amounts of data and recognize patterns that are invisible to the human eye. This helps financial institutions to identify fraudulent activities, and make investment decisions based on more accurate predictions.

In healthcare, generative deep learning can be used to develop personalized treatments for patients, based on their medical history and genetic makeup. This technology can also be used to identify new drugs and treatments that are more effective than existing ones. It is also useful in analyzing medical images such as MRI scans, and can help doctors to detect diseases at an early stage.

In retail, generative deep learning can be used to analyze consumer behavior and predict consumer preferences. This can help retailers to identify trends and develop targeted marketing campaigns. It can also be used to optimize supply chain logistics, to ensure that products are delivered to the right locations at the right time.

It is clear that generative deep learning has the potential to transform the way we live and work. As the technology advances and becomes more widely used, we can expect to see even more innovative applications in a wide range of industries.

10.2.1 Healthcare

Generative models have been widely used in healthcare to generate synthetic patient data that can be used to train other machine learning models. The synthetic data can mimic the characteristics of real patient data, which allows for the development of highly accurate predictive models without the privacy concerns associated with using real patient data.

Generative models can help design new drugs by generating potential chemical compounds and predicting their properties. This can speed up the drug discovery process by reducing the time and cost of manual screening.

Additionally, generative models can be used in medical imaging to enhance image quality, perform image reconstruction, and generate images to augment existing datasets for improved diagnostic models. This is particularly important when dealing with rare diseases or conditions where real patient data is scarce. By generating synthetic data, researchers can train models to detect and diagnose these conditions accurately, which can lead to better patient outcomes.

The use of generative models in healthcare is becoming increasingly important and holds great promise for improving patient care and advancing medical research.

```python
# Example: Using a GAN to generate synthetic medical images
# Note: This is a simplified example, in a real-world scenario you'll need a lar
ger dataset and more complex architectures.

from keras.datasets import mnist
from keras.models import Sequential
from keras.layers import Dense, LeakyReLU, BatchNormalization
from keras.optimizers import Adam
from keras import initializers

# We will use MNIST data as a stand-in for medical images in this example
(X_train, _), (_, _) = mnist.load_data()
X_train = (X_train.astype(np.float32) - 127.5)/127.5
X_train = X_train.reshape(60000, 784)

random_dim = 100

# The generator model
generator = Sequential()
generator.add(Dense(256, input_dim=random_dim, kernel_initializer=initializers.R
andomNormal(stddev=0.02)))
generator.add(LeakyReLU(0.2))
generator.add(BatchNormalization(momentum=0.8))
generator.add(Dense(512))
generator.add(LeakyReLU(0.2))
generator.add(BatchNormalization(momentum=0.8))
generator.add(Dense(1024))
generator.add(LeakyReLU(0.2))
generator.add(BatchNormalization(momentum=0.8))
generator.add(Dense(784, activation='tanh'))

# The discriminator model
discriminator = Sequential()
discriminator.add(Dense(1024, input_dim=784, kernel_initializer=initializers.Ran
domNormal(stddev=0.02)))
discriminator.add(LeakyReLU(0.2))
discriminator.add(Dropout(0.3))
discriminator.add(Dense(512))
discriminator.add(LeakyReLU(0.2))
discriminator.add(Dropout(0.3))
discriminator.add(Dense(256))
discriminator.add(LeakyReLU(0.2))
discriminator.add(Dropout(0.3))
discriminator.add(Dense(1, activation='sigmoid'))

# ... Training code goes here ...
```

Code block 106

10.2.2 Entertainment

The entertainment industry is undoubtedly benefiting from generative models, which have become increasingly popular in the realm of content creation. One of the most exciting applications of these models is the generation of new scripts for movies or TV shows. By utilizing generative models, writers and producers can explore new and innovative storylines, which might not have been possible otherwise.

Generative models have also proven to be useful in creating new pieces of music. By using these models, musicians can experiment with different sounds and styles, which can lead to the creation of entirely new genres of music.

In addition to this, generative models can also be used to create compelling virtual characters for video games or virtual reality experiences. Not only that, but these models are also capable of generating entire virtual worlds, complete with intricate details that would be extremely time-consuming and costly to design by hand.

It is clear that the entertainment industry is just scratching the surface when it comes to the potential applications of generative models in content creation. As technology continues to evolve, it is only a matter of time before we see the full extent of what these models can do.

10.2.3 Finance

In the finance industry, generative models can be used to simulate financial markets, allowing firms to stress-test their portfolios against a wide range of possible market scenarios. Moreover, these models can also be utilized to assess how different financial instruments might perform in various market conditions, providing companies with a better understanding of the potential risks and rewards associated with different investments.

Not only that, but generative deep learning models are also being employed in other industries. In the field of art, for example, these models are being used to create entirely new forms of digital art that were previously impossible. Similarly, in the gaming industry, these models are allowing developers to create more immersive and engaging experiences for players.

In addition, generative models are also helping companies to provide better services to their customers. For instance, these models can be used to generate personalized product recommendations based on a customer's browsing history and past purchases. In the healthcare industry, these models can even be used to design new drugs and treatments by simulating the behavior of molecules and proteins.

As these technologies continue to develop and mature, we can expect to see even more innovative applications of generative deep learning. From improving decision-making to driving innovation, the potential benefits of these models are vast and far-reaching. As such, it is crucial for companies to start exploring these technologies today, to stay ahead of the curve and remain competitive in a rapidly changing business landscape.

In the next section, we will explore ethical considerations associated with the rise of generative deep learning.

10.3 Ethical Considerations in Generative Deep Learning

Generative deep learning is a rapidly evolving and highly promising field. While the technology has enormous potential, it is important to consider the ethical implications of its use. As with any tool, there is always the potential for misuse, and it is incumbent upon researchers, practitioners, and policymakers to ensure that generative deep learning is used ethically and responsibly.

This means considering issues such as privacy, bias, and fairness in the development and deployment of these technologies. Moreover, it is important to recognize that the impacts of generative deep learning are not limited to technical considerations, but also have broader social and economic implications.

As such, it is important to engage in thoughtful and informed discussions about the ethical and societal implications of this technology, and to work together to ensure that its benefits are realized in a way that is equitable and inclusive.

10.3.1 Privacy Concerns

One of the most pressing ethical issues to consider in today's digital landscape is privacy. With the proliferation of increasingly sophisticated generative models, these models are now capable of generating highly realistic and personalized content. This can range from targeted advertisements that cater to an individual's interests, to entirely personalized experiences within digital products that provide a highly tailored user experience.

However, this level of personalization comes at a cost. When generative models have access to a user's personal data, there is a serious risk of generating content that infringes on an individual's privacy. This can manifest in various ways, from the unauthorized sharing of personal information to the creation of synthetic identities that could be used for fraudulent activities.

In addition to the risks posed to individual privacy by generative models, there are also broader societal implications to consider. For instance, the use of generative models in advertising raises questions about the ethics of manipulating consumers with highly personalized content.

Furthermore, the creation of synthetic identities could have far-reaching consequences for society as a whole, potentially undermining the integrity of various institutions that rely on the validity of personal data.

In light of these concerns, it is clear that we need to take a closer look at the ethical implications of generative models and their impact on privacy. While these models undoubtedly have the potential to revolutionize the way we interact with technology, it is important that we do not sacrifice personal privacy and the integrity of personal data in the process.

10.3.2 Misinformation and Deepfakes

Generative deep learning has revolutionized the field of artificial intelligence, enabling the creation of highly realistic fake images, text, and even videos, which are commonly referred to as 'deepfakes'.

These deepfakes are increasingly being used in various fields such as entertainment, journalism, and even education. In the world of entertainment, deepfakes have the potential to allow filmmakers to create new movies featuring deceased actors, giving audiences the opportunity to see their favorite stars on screen once again.

In journalism, deepfakes have the potential to create new ways of storytelling, such as creating virtual interviews with historical figures, or even allowing reporters to embed themselves in dangerous situations without risking their lives. Even in education, deepfakes have the potential to enhance the learning experience by creating interactive virtual simulations of historical events or scientific experiments.

However, while deepfakes have the potential to revolutionize various fields, they also have troubling implications. In particular, the ability to create highly realistic fake content has raised concerns about the potential misuse of this technology, such as the creation of misleading news and propaganda

The ability to create fake videos of public figures saying or doing things they never actually said or did, could have severe political and societal impacts. In addition, deepfakes can also be used for cyberbullying, revenge porn, and other harmful activities. As deepfake technology continues to advance, it is essential that we develop effective methods to detect and combat the misuse of this technology, while still allowing for its positive applications.

Example:

Here's a simple example of how a GPT-2 model can generate human-like text, which can be utilized for both positive and harmful purposes:

```python
# This is a very simplified example. Real-world usage would require more caution
and resources.
from transformers import GPT2LMHeadModel, GPT2Tokenizer

tokenizer = GPT2Tokenizer.from_pretrained("gpt2")
model = GPT2LMHeadModel.from_pretrained("gpt2")

prompt = "In a shocking turn of events, scientists have discovered"
inputs = tokenizer.encode(prompt, return_tensors="pt")
outputs = model.generate(inputs, max_length=100, num_return_sequences=5, tempera
ture=0.7)

for i in range(5):
    print(f"Generated text {i+1}:")
    print(tokenizer.decode(outputs[i], skip_special_tokens=True))
```

Code block 107

10.3.3 Bias in Generative Models

Like all machine learning models, generative models are susceptible to the biases present in the data they are trained on. This can lead to models that perpetuate harmful stereotypes or discriminate against certain groups. It's essential to be aware of these biases and take steps to mitigate them during the model training phase.

One way to mitigate these biases is to carefully select the data used to train the model. This can involve manually reviewing the data to ensure that it is representative of all groups and does not contain any offensive or harmful content. Additionally, techniques such as data augmentation and adversarial training can be used to create a more diverse and balanced training dataset.

Another way to mitigate biases is to use fairness metrics to evaluate the performance of the model. These metrics can help identify any systematic biases in the model's output and guide modifications to the model architecture or training process to reduce these biases.

Finally, it's important to involve diverse stakeholders in the model development process. This can include individuals from underrepresented groups, domain experts, and ethicists. By involving a diverse range of perspectives, it's more likely that biases will be identified and addressed before the model is deployed.

10.4 Social Implications of Generative Deep Learning

As generative deep learning continues to advance and permeate various facets of society, it's important to examine the broader social implications. While it is true that generative deep learning has already made significant contributions in fields such as medicine, transportation, and entertainment, it has the potential to impact even more areas of society.

For instance, in the field of education, generative deep learning could be used to create personalized learning materials for students, based on their individual learning styles and abilities. This could help to improve the overall quality of education and lead to better outcomes for students.

In the field of journalism, generative deep learning could be used to generate news articles and reports, freeing up time for journalists to focus on more in-depth reporting and analysis. However, this also raises concerns about the authenticity and accuracy of the generated content.

Furthermore, in the field of art, generative deep learning could be used to create new forms of visual and audio art, pushing the boundaries of creativity and expression. However, this also raises questions about the role of the artist and the authenticity of the artwork.

While generative deep learning has already made impressive advancements in various fields, it is important to carefully consider its potential impacts on society and to approach its development with caution and responsibility.

10.4.1 Changes in Content Creation

Generative deep learning has the potential to revolutionize the way we create content, ranging from visual arts to written works. Not only can it save time and effort by automating the creative process, but it can also generate completely new and innovative ideas that may not have been thought of otherwise. These tools, such as DALL·E and GPT-3, provide artists and content creators with a much wider range of options and possibilities for their work.

However, with the rise of these tools comes the need to address questions about originality, authenticity, and copyright. While generative deep learning can be a powerful tool for content creation, it is important to consider the ethical implications of using AI to create work that may be seen as derivative or lacking in originality. Additionally, there is also the concern of copyright infringement, as AI-generated content may inadvertently use copyrighted material without proper attribution or permission.

Despite these concerns, the potential benefits of generative deep learning in content creation cannot be ignored. As technology continues to advance, it is important for creators and users alike to consider the ethical implications of using these powerful tools while still embracing their potential to revolutionize the creative process.

10.4.2 Job Displacement and New Opportunities

Just like automation in the industrial sector, advancements in generative models could potentially displace certain jobs, especially those involving repetitive or predictable tasks. For instance, if a machine can write convincing articles or generate engaging social media posts, what becomes of the human writer or social media manager?

It's quite possible that we may see a shift away from traditional forms of content production and towards more automated means. However, it's also important to note that generative deep learning is still in its early stages, and there are many challenges that must be overcome before it can reach its full potential.

On the other hand, new opportunities may arise for those who can leverage these technologies. Just as the rise of the internet created a whole new field of jobs (web design, digital marketing, data science, etc.), generative deep learning could potentially lead to new job categories.

For example, we may see the emergence of "AI trainers" who specialize in fine-tuning generative models to produce specific types of output. Additionally, there may be increased demand for individuals who can interpret and analyze the vast amounts of data generated by these systems, as well as those who can develop and maintain the underlying infrastructure.

10.4.3 Democratizing Creative Tools

Generative deep learning models have the potential to democratize access to creative tools, thereby providing a platform for individuals who lack professional training in areas such as art, music or writing, to create high-quality content.

This could broaden the scope of who can participate in these creative fields, leading to greater diversity in the art and music industry. In addition, generative models can provide a cost-effective solution to traditional creative processes, which can often be expensive and time-consuming. By enabling users to generate high-quality content with minimal effort, generative models may also lead to greater productivity and efficiency in creative endeavors.

Finally, the use of generative models can also result in the development of new and innovative styles, as users experiment with different parameters and settings to create unique and original content. Overall, the potential benefits of generative deep learning models for creative fields are vast and could revolutionize the way we approach art, music, and writing in the future.

10.4.4 Amplifying Online Interactions

Generative models could have a significant impact on the way we interact online. One potential application of these models is the creation of personalized AI-generated responses or content that is tailored specifically to individual users.

This could greatly enhance the online experience by making it more engaging and personalized. However, it is important to consider the potential downsides of such technology. For example, the use of generative models may contribute to the creation of "filter bubbles," where individuals are exposed primarily to content that aligns with their existing beliefs.

This can limit exposure to new ideas and perspectives, which can be detrimental to healthy discourse and decision-making. Additionally, the use of personalized AI-generated content raises privacy concerns, as these models may collect and use personal data to create content tailored to individual users.

It is crucial to carefully consider the ethical implications of generative models in order to ensure that their benefits are maximized while their negative consequences are minimized.

While we've touched on a few potential social implications, the reality is that the full impact of generative deep learning is something that we'll only fully understand as it continues to unfold. As we explore these powerful technologies, it is crucial that we remain mindful of their potential impact and use them in ways that align with our collective values and goals.

10.5 Policy and Regulatory Outlook

As generative deep learning continues to evolve and become more widely used, it is becoming increasingly clear that we need to adapt our policy and regulatory landscape to keep pace with these technological advances. This is particularly important in several key areas, where there are concerns about the impact of this technology on society.

One area of concern is the potential for generative deep learning to be used to create fake or misleading information. This could have serious consequences for our democracy, as it could be used to influence public opinion and sway elections. To address this concern, we may need to consider new regulations or policies that require greater transparency and accountability in the use of this technology.

Another area of concern is the potential for generative deep learning to be used to create highly realistic fake images or videos. This could be used to manipulate or deceive people, and could have serious consequences for individuals and society as a whole. To address this concern, we may need to consider new policies or regulations that restrict the use of this technology in certain contexts, such as political advertising or news reporting.

There is a concern about the impact of generative deep learning on the job market. As this technology becomes more advanced, it has the potential to automate many tasks that are currently performed by humans. This could lead to widespread job loss and economic disruption. To address this concern, we may need to consider policies that support education and job training, and that encourage the development of new industries and job opportunities.

10.5.1 Intellectual Property Rights

One significant area to consider is intellectual property rights. As mentioned previously, generative models have the ability to create art, write articles, generate music, and more. While this technology offers immense potential for innovation, it also raises complex legal questions about ownership and rights to the content generated by these models.

At the heart of this issue is the question of who owns the rights to the content created by generative models. Is it the developer of the model, who designs and builds the software? Or is it the user who inputs the parameters and selects the output? Alternatively, could the AI system itself be considered the creator and therefore the owner of the content?

At present, intellectual property laws are not fully equipped to handle these complexities. While there have been some attempts to address this issue, such as the use of Creative Commons licenses, there is still much work to be done. As generative models become more sophisticated and widespread, it will be increasingly important to develop legal frameworks that balance the interests of creators, developers, users, and society as a whole.

10.5.2 Privacy

Another important issue that has come to the forefront of many discussions is privacy. With many generative models such as those used for generating realistic human faces, being trained on datasets that contain personal information, it has become increasingly important that strict regulations need to be put in place to ensure that this data is anonymized and that individuals' privacy is respected. This means that governments and organizations need to ensure that they are taking all necessary measures to protect people's privacy.

One such policy that has been implemented is the European Union's General Data Protection Regulation (GDPR). This policy has helped to ensure that people's privacy is protected and their personal information is not used without their consent. However, despite the positive effects of the GDPR, many countries still lack robust data privacy laws, leaving individuals vulnerable to data breaches and other privacy violations.

To address this issue, organizations need to take a proactive approach to data privacy. This includes implementing strong data privacy policies, ensuring that all employees are trained on data privacy best practices, and regularly auditing their data handling processes to identify any potential vulnerabilities. By taking these steps, organizations can help to protect people's privacy and prevent data breaches from occurring.

10.5.3 Deepfakes and Misinformation

Generative deep learning has made it much easier to create deepfakes - videos or audio recordings that are so realistic that they can seem real. This technology could be used for malicious purposes, such as spreading false information or defaming individuals.

To prevent these negative impacts, it is important that lawmakers address this issue and develop regulations that define how deepfakes can be used legally and what consequences will be imposed for their unlawful use.

For example, these regulations might include requirements for labeling deepfakes as "simulated content," and prohibiting their use in certain contexts, such as political campaigns or other public discourse. Lawmakers could establish penalties for those who create or distribute deepfakes with harmful intent, such as fines or imprisonment. By taking proactive measures to regulate deepfakes, we can help ensure that this technology is used ethically and safely.

10.5.4 Accountability

Finally, there is the crucial question of accountability in AI-generated content. The matter of responsibility in the event of harm caused by AI is complex, and requires careful consideration. If a piece of content generated by an AI model causes harm, who should be held accountable?

Should it be the creator of the model, the person who utilized it, or the AI itself? This becomes especially intricate when the AI system operates autonomously or semi-autonomously, without the ability for direct human intervention. It is important for us to continually examine and address these complex issues as we move forward with the use of AI in various fields.

10.5.5 Regulatory Bodies

Looking to the future, we might also see the formation of new regulatory bodies dedicated to overseeing the use and development of generative AI technologies. These bodies could play a crucial role in ensuring that the technology is used ethically and safely.

Just like the Food and Drug Administration (FDA) in the US, which oversees the safety and efficacy of pharmaceuticals and medical devices, a similar body could ensure that generative deep learning technologies are used responsibly.

Such a regulatory body could help to prevent the misuse of these technologies, and ensure that they are only used in ways that benefit society. This would involve setting strict guidelines for the development and use of these technologies, as well as monitoring their use to ensure compliance.

By doing so, we can ensure that generative AI technologies are developed and used in a way that is safe, ethical, and beneficial to everyone.

This is by no means an exhaustive list of all the regulatory considerations associated with generative deep learning, but it gives a glimpse of the complexities involved. As we navigate the future of generative deep learning, it will be critical to have policy and regulatory frameworks that promote innovation while also safeguarding societal values and individual rights.

10.6 Future Research Directions

As we wrap up this exploration of generative deep learning, it's fitting that we take some time to look ahead to where the field is headed. Generative models have been shown to be powerful tools for understanding and manipulating complex data, but they are far from a solved problem. Here are some promising directions for future research.

10.6.1 Enhanced Quality and Diversity

One of the primary objectives of any generative model is to produce outputs that are both of high quality and realistic. Although there have been considerable advancements in the quality of the samples generated by deep generative models, particularly in areas such as image and text generation, there is always room for improvement.

There are several avenues for future research in this field, one of which is to ensure that models capture the full diversity of the training data. This is particularly important in avoiding mode collapse, a phenomenon we discussed at length in chapter 9. Mode collapse occurs when the model focuses too much on a few modes of the data and ignores others.

It is a crucial problem to solve because it reduces the overall quality of the output and can make it less representative of the underlying data. Therefore, future research should focus on devising new methods to prevent mode collapse and to ensure that the model can capture the full range of diversity in the training data. By doing so, we can continue to improve the quality and realism of the generated outputs, and push the boundaries of what is possible with generative models.

10.6.2 Interpretable and Controllable Outputs

Generative models have the ability to produce complex data, but the complexity can make it difficult to understand and control what is being generated. As such, future research will likely focus on improving the interpretability of these models. This will make it easier for users to understand how changes in the input affect the output.

A potential research direction is to develop techniques that provide more control over the output without requiring a full retraining of the model. For instance, in a GAN trained to generate images, one might want to understand which aspects of the input noise vector control color, shape, size, and other attributes. By gaining a better understanding of these aspects, researchers can develop techniques that provide more fine-grained control over the final output. This will not only make it easier to achieve the desired output but also provide insight into how the model works and how it can be improved.

10.6.3 Fair and Ethical AI

As we have discussed in the previous sections, generative models have significant and complex societal and ethical implications. However, there is still much research that needs to be done to ensure that these models respect privacy, avoid bias, and are used responsibly.

In order to address these issues, researchers may want to investigate techniques for anonymizing the data that is used to train generative models. This can be a delicate process, but it is important to ensure that the privacy of individuals is respected.

Another important area of research is the development of mechanisms for detecting and mitigating bias in the outputs of generative models. There is a growing concern that these models may unintentionally perpetuate existing biases or even amplify them. Therefore, it is crucial to develop ways to detect and correct any biases that are present in these models.

Lastly, it is important to consider methods for detecting misuse of these technologies. This can include developing algorithms that can detect when generative models are being used for malicious purposes, as well as developing policies and regulations to ensure that these models are only used for ethical and responsible purposes.

The research into generative models and their implications is an ongoing and complex process. However, by investigating techniques for anonymizing data, detecting and mitigating bias, and detecting misuse, we can move towards a future where these models are used in a responsible and ethical manner.

10.6.4 Efficient and Scalable Models

As we move towards more complex data and larger models, research into more efficient and scalable algorithms for training and inference will be important. To achieve these goals, we need to devote resources to a variety of research directions.

One possible avenue of research is the development of new architectures. By experimenting with alternative model structures, we can potentially discover more effective ways to represent complex data. Additionally, new optimization algorithms could help us train these models more efficiently, reducing the time and resources required to achieve high performance.

Another promising area of investigation is hardware design. By developing specialized hardware for generative models, we could potentially achieve significant speedups in training and inference. This could include the development of specialized processors, memory architectures, or other hardware components that are optimized for the specific demands of generative modeling.

There are many exciting research directions that could help us improve the efficiency and scalability of generative models. By investing in these areas, we can ensure that we are well-positioned to tackle the challenges of complex data and large models in the years to come.

10.6.5 Multi-modal Generative Models

Finally, one exciting direction for future research is the development of generative models that can handle multiple modalities of data. This can include audio, visual, textual, and other modalities.

These models can be used for a wide range of applications, such as video generation, speech synthesis, and image captioning. For example, a model might be trained to generate a video (a visual modality) and a corresponding audio track (an audio modality) simultaneously, while also generating a textual description of the content (a textual modality).

This kind of multi-modal learning is a challenging problem and represents an exciting frontier for generative models, as it requires the integration of different types of data and the development of novel architectures and training methods to effectively learn from them.

The potential applications of these models are vast, ranging from entertainment and media to healthcare and education, and the research in this area is sure to yield many exciting breakthroughs in the years to come.

In conclusion, generative deep learning is a vibrant field with numerous opportunities for future research. As we continue to explore this fascinating area, we hope this book will serve as a valuable guide and reference for your journey. We can't wait to see what you'll create!

Chapter 10: Conclusion

It's been an enlightening journey through the world of generative deep learning. This concluding chapter sought to provide a glimpse into the future of the field, focusing on emerging trends, potential impacts across different industries, ethical considerations, societal implications, and policy outlooks. We also highlighted potential areas for future research.

We began with an exploration of emerging trends in generative deep learning, illustrating the fast-paced advancements and improvements in the field. We then moved on to discuss how these developments are expected to impact various industries, demonstrating the versatility and potential of generative models in real-world applications.

Ethical considerations and societal implications were the focus of our subsequent discussions. As with any powerful technology, generative deep learning poses significant ethical questions and societal challenges that need to be navigated with care. It is crucial to ensure these models respect privacy, avoid bias, and are used responsibly.

We then touched upon the policy and regulatory outlook, acknowledging that the pace of technological advancement often outstrips the development of policy and regulation. It is essential to foster an ongoing dialogue between researchers, policymakers, and the public to navigate these challenges effectively.

Finally, we highlighted some exciting directions for future research, including the pursuit of enhanced quality and diversity in outputs, improving interpretability, ensuring fair and ethical AI, developing more efficient models, and exploring multi-modal generative models.

As we close this chapter, we hope that you leave with not just a solid understanding of generative deep learning but also an appreciation for its potential and the complex considerations it invites. As we stand on the precipice of an exciting future in generative deep learning, we hope this book will serve as a compass, helping you navigate the intricate landscape of this fascinating field.

Your journey doesn't stop here; it's only just begun. Here's to the future, a future we look forward to you shaping with your contributions. Happy learning, and happy creating!

Conclusion

And so, we've arrived at the end of our journey, a journey through the intricate and fascinating world of generative deep learning. It has been a remarkable expedition, with the shared purpose of understanding this complex field of artificial intelligence. A path that led us through the fundamental concepts, exploring and delving deep into the core technologies, and then arriving at the cutting-edge advancements and emerging trends shaping the field.

This book has taken you, the reader, through the many facets of generative deep learning, including its theoretical foundations, the broad range of models, and their applications. From simple feed-forward networks, we journeyed to complex convolutional neural networks (CNNs), generative adversarial networks (GANs), variational autoencoders (VAEs), and autoregressive models. We explored both the code and the concepts that bring these models to life, offering you hands-on experience with their implementation and use.

We also dived into several projects, building real-world applications using generative models. The projects aimed to cement your understanding, offer practical insights, and showcase the potential applications of these models. These projects, on image synthesis with GANs, handwritten digit generation with VAEs, and text generation with autoregressive models, are representative of the numerous potential applications in the wide world of generative deep learning.

Through these explorations, we hope to have instilled in you a robust understanding of the essential principles, methodologies, and techniques underlying generative deep learning. An understanding that equips you to apply these concepts to diverse problems and to create solutions that can shape the world.

As we ventured towards the book's conclusion, we also took time to examine the future landscape of generative deep learning. We explored the emerging trends, the potential impacts on various industries, the ethical considerations, societal implications, policy, and regulatory outlooks. These discussions were crucial in painting a comprehensive picture of the field, not just as a technical domain but also as a significant influence on our society and future.

We are standing at the precipice of an era where AI has the potential to redefine many aspects of our lives and society. Generative deep learning models are on the frontline of this transformation. They hold the promise of unprecedented advancements, from creating new forms of art and music to revolutionizing healthcare, climate modelling, and more.

However, with great power comes great responsibility. The ethical considerations and societal implications we discussed are a reminder of this responsibility. As we continue to develop and deploy these models, we need to ensure they are used ethically and responsibly, promoting fairness, inclusivity, and transparency.

Moreover, as the field continues to evolve rapidly, it will inevitably shape and be shaped by the policy and regulatory landscape. It's vital for policymakers, regulators, researchers, and practitioners to engage in ongoing dialogues to navigate the challenges and opportunities presented by these technological advancements.

Looking forward, there's much to be excited about in the realm of generative deep learning. The future research directions we discussed promise to keep the field vibrant and evolving, pushing the boundaries of what's possible. Your journey through this book is a significant step into this future.

In conclusion, we hope this book has served as a guide, a teacher, and a source of inspiration as you navigate the complex yet rewarding landscape of generative deep learning. This journey doesn't end here; in fact, it's only just begun. The field is ripe with opportunities for innovation, and we look forward to your contributions to this exciting domain.

Thank you for accompanying us on this journey. We hope the knowledge and insights gained here will inform your work and inspire you to drive further advancements in generative deep learning. The future is in your hands. Let's create it responsibly, ethically, and innovatively. Onward and upward, to a future shaped by our collective imagination and creativity. Happy learning, and happy creating!

Where to continue?

If you've completed this book, and are hungry for more programming knowledge, we'd like to recommend some other books from our software company that you might find useful. These books cover a wide range of topics and are designed to help you continue to expand your programming skills.

1. **"ChatGPT API Bible: Mastering Python Programming for Conversational AI"**: Provide a hands-on, step-by-step guide to utilizing ChatGPT, covering everything from API integration to fine-tuning the model for specific tasks or industries.
2. **"Natural Language Processing with Python: Building your Own Customer Service ChatBot"**: This expansive book offers an in-depth exploration of NLP. It successfully simplifies complex concepts using engaging explanations and intuitive examples.
3. **"Data Analysis with Python"** - Python is a powerful language for data analysis, and this book will help you unlock its full potential. It covers topics such as data cleaning, data manipulation, and data visualization, and provides you with practical exercises to help you apply what you've learned.
4. **"Machine Learning with Python"** - Machine learning is one of the most exciting fields in computer science, and this book will help you get started with building your own machine learning models using Python. It covers topics such as linear regression, logistic regression, and decision trees.
5. **"Mastering ChatGPT and Prompt Engineering"** - In this book, we will take you on a comprehensive journey through the world of prompt engineering, covering everything from the fundamentals of AI language models to advanced strategies and real-world applications.

All of these books are designed to help you continue to expand your programming skills and deepen your understanding of the Python language. We believe that programming is a skill that can be learned and developed over time, and we are committed to providing resources to help you achieve your goals.

We'd also like to take this opportunity to thank you for choosing our software company as your guide in your programming journey. We hope that you have found this book of Python for beginners to be a valuable resource, and we look forward to continuing to provide you with high-quality programming resources in the future. If you have any feedback or suggestions for future books or resources, please don't hesitate to get in touch with us. We'd love to hear from you!

Know more about us

At Cuantum Technologies, we specialize in building web applications that deliver creative experiences and solve real-world problems. Our developers have expertise in a wide range of programming languages and frameworks, including Python, Django, React, Three.js, and Vue.js, among others. We are constantly exploring new technologies and techniques to stay at the forefront of the industry, and we pride ourselves on our ability to create solutions that meet our clients' needs.

If you are interested in learning more about our Cuantum Technologies and the services that we offer, please visit our website at books.cuantum.tech. We would be happy to answer any questions that you may have and to discuss how we can help you with your software development needs.

www.cuantum.tech

Made in the USA
Monee, IL
07 September 2023